Praise for *Rules for Conservatives*

"Saul Alinsky gave liberals a game plan that they followed for the last 40 years. Rules for Conservatives is the game plan for conservatives to fight against what the liberals have done."
—Jerry Corsi, PhD. (Harvard) and author of **Obamanation, America for Sale**, and **Unfit for Command**

"A dynamic and pow   ou. As in his last book, Save   Master tells it like it is and take   is required reading for all who consider the   to be Conservative."
—V. A. Araneta, CEO of small Hispanic-owned business

"In Rules for Conservatives, Mike Master reminds us that the US Constitution, founded upon the Declaration of Independence, is the most profound, most brilliant blueprint of limited government ever established. It has guided America to become the freest, strongest, most prosperous, and most generous nation in history. To "Save America now" and restore her to greatness, our government must return to our founding principles, and then get out of the way."
—Jack Tymann, retired president of Westinghouse, Chairman of an alternate energy company, Lecturer, Commentator, Tea Party leader, and Political Pundit

"The midnight rides of Paul Revere gave life saving alert to the colonist that the British were coming. Rules for Conservatives is

an eleventh-hour cry to all Americans endangered by Mr. Obama and the Liberal agenda poised to destroy this nation. Michael Charles Master writes with the passion of the Old Testament Priest Samuel who pleaded with Israel to turn from her liberal godless ways. The Colonists heard Paul Revere and the nation was saved. If we hear the pleadings and instructions in this sacred document, America will be likewise saved."

—James David Manning,

Pastor of the Church of Atlah in New York City

"Mike is a serious observer of politics and a very patriotic American. His latest book provides clear solutions to the problems he sees facing America. Mike has been a guest lecturer in several of my classes and I admire his enthusiasm and work ethic as a political writer/researcher and successful businessman. "

—Guy DeRosa, Professor of Political Science, Mercer County Community College

Rules for Conservatives

Rules for
CONSERVATIVES

A Response to

Rules for Radicals by Saul Alinsky

Michael Charles Master

Rules for Conservatives © 2012 by Michael Charles Master

For information regarding sales or licensing, please contact the publisher:
Dunham Books
63 Music Square East
Nashville, Tennessee 37203
www.dunhamgroupinc.com

Trade Paperback Edition: ISBN 978-0-9837456-8-6
 E-book Edition: 978-0-9839-9060-4

First printing February, 2012
Second printing April, 2012

Printed in the United States of America

Dedication

There was a time when you could tell the good guys from the bad guys because the good guys wore white hats and rode white horses. Now that the bad guys have learned to disguise themselves in the white hats and white horses of "social justice," "helping the less fortunate," "political correctness," and "one world order," it is important for the rest of us to recognize the bad guys by other means than just looking at their hats and horses … and then we need to fight them with all of our might.

This book is dedicated to each American who wants to know what to do to fight against the destruction of America by liberal radicals.

John 5:36: *"Doing the work of the one who sent me."*

Table of Contents

Foreword

Mike Master introduced himself to me at our church, St. Luke's Catholic Church in McLean, Virginia, at a 6:45 AM Mass one weekday morning in 2000. I was the chairman of the RNC at the time when George W. Bush was running for president. Mike listened to me ask the priest why the Catholic Church was being so silent about abortion, euthanasia and gay marriage. He wrote about that conversation in his first book, *Save America Now*.

America faces some very difficult challenges. The retirement of so many baby boom workers over the next 20 years, without enough younger workers to replace them will place an enormous strain on Social Security revenues vs. expenses, on Medicare costs, and on the economy. The high number of people retiring without enough younger people replacing them is decreasing the demand for goods, is reducing the demand for housing, and is depleting our brain trust of intelligence/experience. The huge amounts of immigration for the previous 20 years is changing the culture of America as more immigrants are used to offset the lack of births to American citizens. The huge increases to the number of government workers in the federal government and local governments, and the high levels of pay for those workers are causing record deficits to our federal and local governments. The loss of manufacturing to more cost effective foreign manufacturers continues to cause more unemployment to American workers. The low level of science and engineering graduates vs. liberal arts graduates is making America weaker. The high level of dependence on foreign oil is draining capital from America. And the threats from enemies to America are real and are increasing.

Saul Alinsky wrote Rules for Radicals 40 years ago as instructions on how to seize power. Alinsky was the original community organizer who documented how to organize others to provide power to the organizers. Because of those who practiced those "rules," America is suffering. Alinsky instructed radical liberal leaders to organize masses to force the government to compromise with them. Every one of the problems that Americans face today can be traced back to compromises with liberal radical leaders over the last 40 years.

Mike Master wrote Rules for Conservatives as the counter strategy to Rules for Radicals. It is common sense and practical. It provides actions that each one of us can do every day. It provides instructions to conservatives on how to stop the erosion of America's values, economy, culture, and life style by the liberal radicals.

—Robert James (Jim) Nicholson

Jim Nicholson is a 1961 graduate of the United States Military Academy at West Point, served in the Vietnam War where he earned the Bronze Star , retired in 1991 with the rank of Colonel and earned a law degree from the University of Denver in 1972. He is a lawyer and an entrepreneur and custom home builder. He served as Chairman of the Republican National Committee 1997 – 2001, Ambassador to the Vatican, Secretary of US Veterans Affairs, and is currently Senior Counsel at Brownstein Hyatt Farber Schreck .

Introduction

Rules for Conservatives is my second step in the war to save America. *Save America Now* was written in 2009 as the first of my two steps in the war to save America from destruction by liberal socialist tyrants. Like the profits from *Save America Now*, the profits of *Rules for Conservatives* are sent to a church in Harlem, New York because religion is one of those critical items needed to save America.

Save America Now is a description of the most destructive enemies within our country. It is a statement about what those enemies want to destroy. It is a discussion of history and the cycles that are working against the survival of the American dream as defined by our Founding Fathers. It is a list as to "what" needs to be saved. And it is a plan as to "what" needs to be done to *save America now*.

Rules for Conservatives assumes that the reader is familiar with the issues and plans in Save America Now while *Rules for Conservatives* discusses "how" to implement the plans.

Free enterprise is the foundation of freedom. Private ownership of assets is the direct result of free enterprise. Clearly, our Founding Fathers meant for government to protect free enterprise and private ownership. While exercising free enterprise, corporations sometimes abuse citizens. So, our Founding Fathers established a government to protect the citizens of America from abuses by corporations. The conflict between protecting free enterprise/private ownership and protecting citizens from corporate abuse has been used by government to grow itself. But government is just as much an abuser of power as any other enemy to freedom. So in reality, corporations and citizens need to be protected from government. Therefore, our Founding Fathers also gave us a road map for protection from government. It is the Constitution of the United States. It is the contract between "we the people" and our federal government which places limits on the authority and scope of the federal government.

The Constitution contains the terms and conditions of how to implement the mission statement in our Declaration of Independence. The Declaration of Independence as written by Thomas Jefferson is the mission statement for America. It is the dream for our country. It gave birth to America.

It states:

> *When in the Course of human events, it becomes necessary for one people to dissolve the political bands which have connected them with another, and to assume among the powers of the earth, the separate and equal station to which the Laws of Nature and of Nature's God entitle them, a descent respect to the opinions of mankind requires that they should declare the causes which impel them to the separation...*
>
> *We hold these truths to be self-evident:*
>
> *That all men are created equal; that they are endowed by their Creator with certain unalienable rights; that among these are life, liberty, and the pursuit of happiness; that, to secure these rights, governments are instituted among men,*

deriving their just powers from the consent of the governed; that whenever any form of government becomes destructive of these ends, it is the right of the people to alter or to abolish it, and to institute new government,

....We, therefore, the Representatives of the united States of America, in General Congress, Assembled, appealing to the Supreme Judge of the world for the rectitude of our intentions, do, in the Name, and by Authority of the good People of these Colonies, solemnly publish and declare, That these United Colonies are, and of Right ought to be Free and Independent States; that they are Absolved from all Allegiance to the British Crown, and that all political connection between them and the state of Great Britain, is and ought to be totally dissolved; and that as Free and Independent States, they have full Power to levy War, conclude Peace, contract Alliances, establish Commerce, and to do all other Acts and Things which Independent States may of right do.

—And for the support of this Declaration, with a firm reliance on the protection of divine Providence, we mutually pledge to each other our Lives, our fortunes and our sacred Honor.

Let's look at that mission statement (Declaration of Independence) more closely: "When in the Course of human events, it becomes necessary for one people to dissolve the political bands which have connected them with another...." is a clear statement that it is necessary at times for people to dissolve those ties they have with others—especially with governments." And to assume among the powers of the earth, the separate and equal station to which the Laws of Nature and of Nature's God entitle them" is also a clear statement that our Founding Fathers built their premise for the mission of America on a belief that there is a God and that our stations in life are equal in nature as determined by God—not by man.

"That all men are created equal" is the foundation for freedom. It states that we start life from the same act of creation. It does not say that we are the same, or that we should be the same, or that we should obtain the same results from our actions. It just states that we are equal in how we were created.

"That they are endowed by their Creator with certain unalienable rights; that among these are life, liberty, and the pursuit of happiness;" states our rights and that how we attained those rights were from God. Any other items granted by a society are privileges of being in that society ... not rights. And from that creation, we are free to pursue our own definitions of happiness without restrictions or guarantees to achieving that happiness as long as it does not harm others. It is clear that these "rights" come from the Creator, God, and therefore cannot be diminished or changed by man—not even by a majority vote.

This is the key to America: God, not man, gave us our rights. Therefore, any man or group of men in the form of government or any other types of organizations who try to change those rights by either increasing or decreasing them, are in defiance of the unalienable rights given to each of us by God.

> *If men can give benefits or rights to other men, then those same men who grant such benefits can also take away rights and benefits and can also grant those benefits or rights based on political reasons.*

Therefore, our Founding Fathers were careful to define those rights, which are not negotiable as being unalienable rights from God, the creator... not subject to the whims of man.

"To secure these rights, governments are instituted among men, deriving their just powers from the consent of the governed;" is the mission statement for government. The responsibility of government in the USA is to secure the rights for the citizens as stated in this Declaration. Governments are made up of men who are to protect those rights that are ordained from God. It is not the job of men in government to define rights. It is their job to protect the rights as defined by God.

"That whenever any form of government becomes destructive of these ends, it is the right of the people to alter or to abolish it, and to institute new government," clearly states that the government is accountable to the people. People have standing, and if the government ignores this fact, then the people need to do what is necessary to take back the country from the government. The colonists took the extreme position of abolishing the British controlled government in America.

"....We, therefore, the Representatives of the united States of America, in General Congress, Assembled, appealing to the Supreme Judge of the world for the rectitude of our intentions," is another statement of how the Founding Fathers were so aware of their relationship to the "Supreme Judge," God.

"Do, in the Name, and by Authority of the good People of these Colonies, solemnly publish and declare, That these United Colonies are, and of Right ought to be Free and Independent States; that they are Absolved from all Allegiance to the British Crown, and that all political connection between them and the state of Great Britain, is and ought to be totally dissolved;"

is another key to the thinking of our Founding Fathers. The Declaration of Independence is a statement of "independence." It is not a declaration of co-dependence or inter-dependence or any other dilution of "independence." The U.S. Declaration of Independence is a definition of individual rights, not group rights, not villages, not unions, not any other form of organization other than "independence."

Those politicians who see America as a dependent member of a world order are in direct opposition to this statement of independence by our Founding Fathers.

"That they are Absolved from all Allegiance to the British Crown, and that all political connection between them and the state of Great Britain, is and ought to be totally dissolved; and that as Free and Independent States, they have full Power to levy War, conclude Peace, contract Alliances, establish Commerce, and to do all other Acts and Things which Independent States may of right do." The states were meant to be independent states. As such, the Constitution takes its mission from this document and defines how to maintain independence when it levies war, concludes peace, contracts alliance, establishes commerce, and does all other acts and things which independent statesmay have the right to do. Since this comment is so encompassing, the founding fathers included ten immediate amendments to the Constitution called the Bill of Rights to limit the scope of the federal government. The tenth states: "The powers not delegated to the United States by the Constitution, nor prohibited by it to the States, are reserved to the States respectively, or to the people."

Then the Declaration concludes with: "And for the support of this Declaration, with a firm reliance on the protection of divine Providence, we mutually pledge to each other our Lives, our fortunes and our sacred Honor."

Oh my! How many of our leaders today would take such a pledge? How many of our current political leaders would sign such a document with such a pledge?

Let's compare that mission statement as defined in the Declaration of Independence to the Constitution of the United States. The Constitution is the organization and procedures to be used by government to implement the mission stated in the Declaration. The Constitution is the contract between "we the people" and our government as to the limitations of government, and how the federal government is meant to be accountable to "we the people." The topics in the Constitution define the organization, rules, and the process of the federal government. The Constitution defines the domain of the federal government and the domain of the individual states. It clearly states in the Tenth Amendment that anything that is not deliberately delegated to the federal government in the Constitution is the domain of the states and/or the people. This is the list of articles and amendments in the Constitution.

Preamble
Article 1—The Legislative Branch
Section 1—The Legislature
Section 2—The House
Section 3—The Senate
Section 4—Elections, Meetings
Section 5—Membership, Rules, Journals, Adjournment
Section 6—Compensation
Section 7—Revenue Bills, Legislative Process, Presidential Veto
Section 8—Powers of Congress
Section 9—Limits on Congress

with our government called the Constitution of the United States
Special interest groups control the government. They c
three branches. They have more influence on
than the influence of "we the people"

Those enemies to freed
in *Save America No*
America No
and th

T
stopping
Radicals (S
use to impl
by liberals in
that conservati
by liberals. It is a
nation that our F
Independence and

Since the begin
the Tea Parties. TEA st
movement is determine
Without increased tax re
stop. With decreased tax re
shrink itself.

Reducing taxes and reducing governme
keys to stopping the growth to government–the local, feder
educational system—all government. Without i
governments lose power.

The Republican and the Democ
dismissed the Tea Parties. Democrats trie
as racists. Republicans tried to label them a

11

Amendment 15—Race No Bar to Vote
Amendment 16—Status of Income Tax Clarified
Amendment 17—Senators Elected by Popular Vote
Amendment 18—Liquor Abolished
Amendment 19—Women's Suffrage
Amendment 18, Congressional Terms
Amendment 20—Presidential, Congressional Terms
Amendment 21—Amendment 18 Repealed
Amendment 22—Presidential Term Limits
Amendment 23—Presidential Vote for District of Columbia
Amendment 24—Poll Taxes Barred
Amendment 25—Presidential Disability and Succession
Amendment 26—Voting Age Set to 18 Years
Amendment 27—Limiting Changes to Congressional Pay

It is important to note that the articles and amendments of the
Constitution are concerned with organization, powers, and
Constitution on those powers. It is also important to note that the
or limits on the Constitution of the United States.
oath taken by our elected officials (I) will to the best of my ability, preserve,
Constitution states: "(I) will to the best of my ability, preserve,
protect and defend the Constitution, traitors to America. And if
Any government as stated in the Constitution, traitors to their
or procedures to the Constitution should abuse the contract with "we the
oaths, traitors to the Constitution who abuse those limitations, rules,
the entire government becomes destructive
people," then the Declaration of Independence instructs us:

"That whenever any form of government becomes destructive
of these ends, it is the right of the people to alter or to abolish it
and to institute new government"

Our federal government
people." *Save America Now* details the a
that the federal government assumes auth
to it in the Constitution. It is doing it by t

9

...the Constitution by activist definitions of the limitations placed on the federal government in the Constitution.

The fifth article in the US Constitution clearly states how the Constitution can be amended. It has been used twenty-seven times to amend the Constitution. So those who redefine the words of the Constitution and assume powers that are not specifically defined in it by claiming that it is a "living document" without using Article V to amend it are clearly in violation of the due process for amending this contract between "we the people" and our government. And that is treason as defined in Article III, Section 3 of the Constitution.

All three branches of the federal government are guilty. The legislative branch passes laws that are outside of the mission in the Declaration and outside the limitations placed on the federal government in the Constitution. The executive branch passes laws that are outside of the mission in the Constitution and outside the limitations placed on the federal government in the Constitution. The executive branch abuses by not using its veto power and by passing legislation that gives it more power and by using legislation that gives it more power and by use of executive power that... The executive branch also implement rules... judicial...

elections in 2010 proved that a large portion of Americans now associate their beliefs more with the Tea Parties than with the political parties, so Democrats and Republicans can no longer marginalize the movement. The Tea Parties are determined to reduce the impact of government on our lives. They are determined to restore the Declaration of Independence and the Constitution of the USA as the controlling documents for our government. If the Tea Party movement can be kept out of the control of Republicans and Democrats, it might just be what is needed to save America.

The Declaration of Independence tells us why America is what it is and what America is meant to be while the Constitution details the process of how American government is supposed to act. Deviations to that process are violations to the contract between "we the people" and our government. That is treason.

Saul Alinsky made this comment to the radical liberals in America in *Rules for Radicals*:

> *... there has always been the enemy within, the hidden and malignant inertia that foreshadows more certain destruction to our life than any nuclear warhead. There can be no darker or more devastating tragedy than the death of a man's faith in himself and in his power to direct his future.*

Saul Alinsky meant for those words to motivate radicals, liberals. Today, these words should mean more to conservatives than to liberals. Conservatives must take action. Conservatives must be involved. Or conservatives will be subjugated to just paying the bills for big liberal government. Then conservatives will become serfs of this next millennium.

Chapter 1
Rules for Radicals by Saul Alinsky

Why is it important to understand the impact of Saul Alinsky and his *Rules for Radicals?*

On the back cover of the most recent printing of *Rules for Radicals,* the *Chicago Sun-Times* makes this comment:

> *Alinsky's techniques and teachings influenced generations of community and labor organizers, including the church-based group hiring a young (Barack) Obama to work on Chicago's South Side in the 1980s....Alinsky impressed a young (Hillary) Clinton, who was growing up in Park Ridge at the time Alinsky was the director of the Industrial Areas Foundation in Chicago.*

Alinsky's techniques are used by labor union leaders, community organizers, Barack Hussein Obama, Hillary Clinton, and many other liberal leaders.

Saul Alinsky was the original "community organizer" in the USA. He was a liberal Jew who made a living by organizing groups of people in his war against the established Christian white communities in America. He was part of the intellectual elite. He was educated at the University of Chicago. He goaded the less fortunate into demanding more from society and gave rules or tactics to them to extort more and more from the producers in the nation. He used envy to motivate communities. He taught them to covet. That gave socialist leaders more political power in the process. And so he wrote *Rules for Radicals* in 1971 as the cookbook for liberals on how they could take control.

In the very first chapter of *Rules for Radicals,*
Alinsky used a quote from the Old Testament, it
states. "The life of man upon earth is warfare."

He continues: "*The Prince* was written by Mac
the Haves on how to hold power. *Rules for Radicals*
for the Have Nots on how to take it away. What follo
those who want to change the world from what it is to w
believe it should be. In this book we are concerned with
create mass organizations to seize power...."

Saul Alinsky was an instigator of class warfare. He w
Instigator of the culture war. He taught liberals how to di
America by organizing communities to seize power.

Saul Alinsky cloaked his instructions in comments abou
his loyalty to the USA. He used the writings of our Founding
Fathers, the Declaration of Independence, and the Constitution
to justify his instructions. He used the rules of our own society
against us ... just as he instructed his readers to do: "use their
own rules against them.' Alinsky divided society into three
groups, the "Haves," the "Have Nots," and the ones who are in
between the Haves and Have Nots who Alinsky calls the 'Have-
a-Little, Want Mores." His objective was clear: take power away
from the capitalist Haves and give it to socialist leaders. His
strategy was also clear.

> *Organize the Have-Nots into fighting against the Haves.*
>
> *Convince those who Want More that they will gain
> more by joining forces with the Have-Nots.*
> *And in the process, add power to those liberals who lead
> the effort.*

Amendment 15—Race No Bar to Vote
Amendment 16—Status of Income Tax Clarified
Amendment 17—Senators Elected by Popular Vote
Amendment 18—Liquor Abolished
Amendment 19—Women's Suffrage
Amendment 20—Presidential, Congressional Terms
Amendment 21—Amendment 18 Repealed
Amendment 22—Presidential Term Limits
Amendment 23—Presidential Vote for District of Columbia
Amendment 24—Poll Taxes Barred
Amendment 25—Presidential Disability and Succession
Amendment 26—Voting Age Set to 18 Years
Amendment 27—Limiting Changes to Congressional Pay

It is important to note that the articles and amendments of the Constitution are concerned with organization, powers, and/or limits on those powers. It is also important to note that the oath taken by our elected officials as defined for them on the Constitution states: "(I) will to the best of my ability, preserve, protect and defend the Constitution of the United States."

Any government leaders who abuse those limitations, rules, or procedures as stated in the Constitution are traitors to their oaths, traitors to the Constitution, traitors to America. And if the entire government should abuse the contract with "we the people," then the Declaration of Independence instructs us:

> *"That whenever any form of government becomes destructive of these ends, it is the right of the people to alter or to abolish it, and to institute new government"*

Our federal government is abusing its responsibility to "we the people." *Save America Now* details the abuses. The most grievous is that the federal government assumes authority that is not granted to it in the Constitution. It is doing it by the loose interpretation of the Constitution by activist definitions of the limitations placed on the federal government in the Constitution.

The fifth article in the US Constitution clearly states how the Constitution can be amended. It has been used twenty-seven times to amend the Constitution. So those who redefine the words of the Constitution and assume powers that are not specifically defined in it by claiming that it is a "living document" without using Article V to amend it are clearly in violation of the due process for amending this contract between "we the people" and our government. And that is treason as defined in Article III, Section 3 of the Constitution.

All three branches of the federal government are guilty. The legislative branch passes laws that are outside of the mission in the Declaration and outside the limitations placed on the federal government in the Constitution. The executive branch allows such abuse by not using its veto power and by encouraging legislation that gives it more power than stipulated in the Constitution. The executive branch exacerbates the problem by use of executive orders and by having executive agencies implement rules that bypass the legislative process. And the judicial branch stretches the meanings of the limitations in the Constitution to allow such abuses.

Who do "we the people" ask for help when the judicial branch and our elected representatives are part of the problem? Who will protect the interests of "we the people" when all three branches of the federal government are in violation of the Constitution?

Why do all three branches allow this? All three branches are the government. All three are protecting each other. No one is protecting the interests of "we the people" in the contract with our government called the Constitution of the United States. Special interest groups control the government. They control all three branches. They have more influence on the government than the influence of "we the people."

Those enemies to freedom and their supporters are defined in *Save America Now*. The supporting evidence is profound. *Save America Now* also defines what needs to be done in the short run and the long run. It was my first step at helping save America.

This book, *Rules for Conservatives*, is my second step at stopping the internal enemies of American citizens. As *Rules for Radicals* (Saul Alinsky, 1971) defined the rules that radicals should use to implement socialism, and more control of government by liberals in America, *Rules for Conservatives* defines the rules that conservatives should use to stop this incremental takeover by liberals. It is a set of rules for reviving the foundations of the nation that our Founding Fathers gave us - the Declaration of Independence and the Constitution of the United States.

Since the beginning of 2009, a phenomenon has occurred: the Tea Parties. TEA stands for Taxed Enough Already. Tea Party movement is determined to cut the tax burden on Americans. Without increased tax revenues, the growth to government will stop. With decreased tax revenues, the government will have to shrink itself.

Reducing taxes and reducing government revenue are the keys to stopping the growth to government–the local, federal, educational system—all government. Without income, all governments lose power.

The Republican and the Democratic parties originally dismissed the Tea Parties. Democrats tried to label the members as racists. Republicans tried to label them as fringe elements. The elections in 2010 proved that a large portion of Americans now associate their beliefs more with the Tea Parties than with the political parties, so Democrats and Republicans can no longer marginalize the movement. The Tea Parties are determined to reduce the impact of government on our lives. They are determined to restore the Declaration of Independence and the Constitution of the USA as the controlling documents for our government. If the Tea Party movement can be kept out of the control of Republicans and Democrats, it might just be what is needed to save America.

The Declaration of Independence tells us why America is what it is and what America is meant to be while the Constitution details the process of how American government is supposed to act. Deviations to that process are violations to the contract between "we the people" and our government. That is treason.

Saul Alinsky made this comment to the radical liberals in America in *Rules for Radicals*:

> ... *there has always been the enemy within, the hidden and malignant inertia that foreshadows more certain destruction to our life than any nuclear warhead. There can be no darker or more devastating tragedy than the death of a man's faith in himself and in his power to direct his future.*

Saul Alinsky meant for those words to motivate radicals, liberals. Today, these words should mean more to conservatives than to liberals. Conservatives must take action. Conservatives must be involved. Or conservatives will be subjugated to just paying the bills for big liberal government. Then conservatives will become the serfs of this next millennium.

Chapter 1
Rules for Radicals by Saul Alinsky

Why is it important to understand the impact of Saul Alinsky and his *Rules for Radicals?*

On the back cover of the most recent printing of *Rules for Radicals,* the *Chicago Sun-Times* makes this comment:

> *Alinsky's techniques and teachings influenced generations of community and labor organizers, including the church-based group hiring a young (Barack) Obama to work on Chicago's South Side in the 1980s....Alinsky impressed a young (Hillary) Clinton, who was growing up in Park Ridge at the time Alinsky was the director of the Industrial Areas Foundation in Chicago.*

Alinsky's techniques are used by labor union leaders, community organizers, Barack Hussein Obama, Hillary Clinton, and many other liberal leaders.

Saul Alinsky was the original "community organizer" in the USA. He was a liberal Jew who made a living by organizing groups of people in his war against the established Christian white communities in America. He was part of the intellectual elite. He was educated at the University of Chicago. He goaded the less fortunate into demanding more from society and gave rules or tactics to them to extort more and more from the producers in the nation. He used envy to motivate communities. He taught them to covet. That gave socialist leaders more political power in the process. And so he wrote *Rules for Radicals* in 1971 as the cookbook for liberals on how they could take control of America.

In the very first chapter of *Rules for Radicals*, "The Purpose," Alinsky used a quote from the Old Testament, Job 7:1, which states: "The life of man upon earth is warfare."

He continues: "*The Prince* was written by Machiavelli for the Haves on how to hold power. *Rules for Radicals* is written for the Have-Nots on how to take it away. What follows is for those who want to change the world from what it is to what they believe it should be. In this book we are concerned with how to create mass organizations to seize power...."

Saul Alinsky was an instigator of class warfare. He was an instigator of the culture war. He taught liberals how to divide America by organizing communities to seize power.

Saul Alinsky cloaked his instructions in comments about his loyalty to the USA. He used the writings of our Founding Fathers, the Declaration of Independence, and the Constitution to justify his instructions. He used the rules of our own society against us ... just as he instructed his readers to do: "use their own rules against them." Alinsky divided society into three groups: the "Haves," the "Have-Nots," and the ones who are in between the Haves and Have-Nots who Alinsky calls the "Have-a-Little, Want Mores." His objective was clear: take power away from the capitalist Haves and give it to socialist leaders. His strategy was also clear:

> *Organize the Have-Nots into fighting against the Haves.*
> *Convince those who Want More that they will gain more by joining forces with the Have-Nots.*
> *And in the process, add power to those liberals who lead the effort.*

Since conservatives tended to have, they were painted as the enemy to the Have-Nots and to those who Want More.

The concepts that were presented by Saul Alinsky to seize power have been practiced by liberals for the last fifty years in their war against conservatives in the U.S. class warfare. Envy. Coveting. Government sponsored theft.

Liberal community organizers created mass organizations to fight conservatives, while conservatives relied on the individual to fight back. While a conservative might say, "The individual and the family are the most important," the liberal will say, "It takes a village."

The result is that liberals are winning. They practice this simple axiom from the *Art of War*: "He who has the largest army will win the war." Liberal leaders have learned to use mass organizations to gain power for themselves.

Liberal leaders control the agenda of America by controlling the largest mass organizations in America ... unions, teachers, media, employees of the federal and local governments, Congress, and the courts. They disguise themselves as Republicans and Democrats, but they are radical liberal leaders. All of them.

In his book, *The Ruling Class*, Angelo M. Codevilla makes the point that Republican leaders and Democrat leaders are much the same. They put on a good show of being in disagreement, but in reality, they are really all of the same ruling class. They differ in who they owe favors, but are the same in growing government. They placate us into thinking that someone is representing the conservative position of shrinking government, when in reality, everything that they do is fixed in advance much like how professional wrestling is fixed before the fight. They make deals with each other and act like they disagree rather than have anyone represent conservatives. So it is naïve to think that conservatives can sit back and let our elected representatives fight for us. We must do it ourselves.

To fight back, conservatives need to understand what those socialists, those liberals, have done—and are doing. Conservatives need to understand what Saul Alinsky taught community organizers to do in *Rules for Radicals*.

The rules presented by Alinsky are really his tactics in the war of liberals against conservatives … against the "white Christian culture." Those rules are the actions to be used, as well as the philosophies behind the actions. So let's discuss some of the most profound rules that Alinsky proposed.

The Ideology of Change

Saul Alinsky: "He (the community organizer) does not have a fixed truth—truth to him is relative and changing."

The objective of the radical is change. It does not matter from what or to what. The objective is change. Without causing change, there is no need and no justification for the community organizer. He points out that the community organizer is not interested in political ideology. The organizer is interested in power, and that power is gained through promoting change. If the society is black, then change it to white. If the society says "yes," then teach it to say "no." The implementation of change provides power to those who lead the effort. And power is the objective—not any specific ideology.

Let me add that "change" is both a noun and a verb. While the objective might be change (a noun), the act of change is a verb: change this or change that. Change as a verb is action.

It grabs the imagination. It causes followers to act blindly just because of being part of "changing" something. To Alinsky and radicals, change is the ideology. Right or wrong, change provides power. And all that matters to the community organizer is how to seize power. Radicals seize power in the process of promoting change; any change.

What change was promised in the 2008 election? None was really defined. Problems with healthcare, financial organizations, and the economy were highlighted to stir up the "Have-nots" and the "Want-Mores," but the solutions encapsulated by the word "change" were vague—other than to close Gitmo and get out of Iraq within a year, of which neither was done within two years following the 2008 election. Change was sold. And change was bought. Change is the real ideology of radicals and community organizers. Any change that can justify their existence is a change that can provide more power to them.

Of Means and Ends

Saul Alinsky: "Does this particular end justify this particular means?"

So many of us have been taught - especially by religious teachings - the end does not justify the means. Saul Alinsky instructs radicals to throw out that concept. He clearly states, "The means-and-end moralists or non-doers always wind up on their ends without any means."

To Saul Alinsky, not only does the end justify the means, but winning justifies anything and everything. The radical, the community organizer, must use a value system that eliminates a moral conscience in order to seize power from those who have it. All actions must be fair game, depending on the particular end. You would not kill someone to win a baseball game (that particular end would not justify the means), but you might threaten to kill a family member of a judge to stop that judge from ruling against you and/or your cause.

Lying? No big deal if it helps accomplish the objective of seizing power. Has anyone stopped to ask why seventeen different judges refused to hear the case concerning the natural born status of Barack Hussein Obama? Did anyone stop to ask why Judge Carter in California rejected the case after he specifically stated that he would hear the case? The case was in front of Carter for two months when he rejected it. He suddenly did an about face and said that only the Washington, DC court had jurisdiction. But in reality, he was aware of the jurisdiction issue for months before he made his statement that he would hear the case. So what really changed? Did someone threaten him? Did someone threaten one of his family members? Did someone bribe him?

There are many Americans who just cannot conceive of such lack of conscience that would permit the end to justify the means. And those same Americans are the ones that Alinsky describes as the "means-and-end moralists who wind up on their ends without any means."

Those moralists are fair game to the community organizer.

Have you seen the 2010 movie, *The Edge of Darkness?* The star, Mel Gibson, is a Boston policeman. During one scene in the kitchen, his police friend implies that Gibson's children will be hurt if he does not do what the bad guys want him to do.

Do you think this only happens in the movies? Real bad guys do really bad things. Do you remember the Russian intelligence officer who died in a UK hospital from radiation poisoning?

What would you do if evil threatened harm to your children or your grandchildren?

Woody is 5 feet 9 inches, stocky, a bit overweight, balding, a veteran, and one tough guy. He told me this story as we sat in his daughter's kitchen in Greenville, South Carolina…Several years ago, on a work assignment where he managed a manufacturing plant in Iran for a large U.S. corporation, three Muslim young men broke into his home one night. As one young man held a revolver against the temple of his infant daughter, another demanded that Woody give him all of his money and his weapons or they would kill his daughter. Woody could sacrifice his own life, but not the life of his daughter. He knew that these were evil men. They were terrorists.

What would you have done if you were Woody?

Woody explained that terrorists attack civilian populations to get those civilians to force the military to surrender. They threaten death to family members to get obedience. They do not attack a brave man directly. Instead, they attack those who the brave man loves to get his compliance.

Now think about those stories concerning the tactics used by ACORN to intimidate banks into giving house mortgages to people who could not pay for them. ACORN was a community organizer.

So why did seventeen different judges refuse to hear the case about the natural born citizenship of Obama? Why did all media refuse to investigate this issue, including FOX?

Judge Carter in California, all judges, the media, and administrators are vulnerable to such threats. How hard would it be for a judge to look at Obama's long form birth certificate, his passports, and his college documents to put an end to the Obama natural born citizenship debate? Why didn't at least one of them do it? Why was Obama not transparent about this? What was he hiding?

At the end of April 2011, Barack Hussein announced on TV that he was making his "birth certificate" available. He was doing it to put an end to the debate about his birth "site." This announcement appeared to be in reaction to the actions of Donald Trump concerning Obama's birth certificate. So the following letter was sent to Mr. Trump from me:

Mr. Donald Trump
725 Fifth Ave.
New York, New York 10022   *May 2, 2011*

Dear Mr. Trump,

While your efforts to obtain the birth certificate of Barack Hussein Obama are to be commended, they also took the attention off the correct subject. Hopefully, you did not do that on purpose. That would make you part of the Obama conspirator organization and complicit in his violations to our Constitution.

This issue is not about where Obama was born. This issue is about his citizenship. Did Obama ever hold a dual citizenship or foreign citizenship that he accepted as an adult? If he ever had a foreign or dual citizenship as an adult, then he is not qualified to be president of the USA.

As the new COLB (certificate of live birth) points out, his father, Obama Sr., was a citizen from Kenya. So

Barack's father was not an American citizen. Therefore, by this very document produced and endorsed by Barack Hussein Obama, he admits that he inherited Kenya citizenship from his father.

Please note that once again Obama did not produce a "birth certificate." He produced another certificate of live birth (COLB). A birth certificate and a COLB are two completely different documents. And once again, Obama and the media are trying to demean those who are questioning Obama's qualifications to serve as president as "radicals" by stating that "now Obama has proved where he was born."

The media constantly kept saying that this issue is about where Obama was born. They kept trying to frame the debate as being about Obama's birthplace ... and you helped them ... while birth place is only part of the issue. But because of how Obama and the media framed this, any more discussion is seen as radical and racially motivated. You either played into their hands or you conspired to help them. So are you a fool or a conspirator?

The real issue is not being addressed. And that real issue is this: did Obama ever use foreign citizenship as an adult? If he did, then he disqualified himself from being able to be president of the United States according to 8 USC 1481 which states that natural born status is lost if the person has become naturalized in another country.

A citizen of the USA can hold dual citizenship. But the office of president, and only the office of president, disallows any person after the original people alive at the time of the signing of the Constitution from ever having a dual or foreign citizenship and be able to be president.

From this new document produced by Obama on April

27, 2001, we know that his father was a Kenyan who passed Kenya citizenship and/or British citizenship to Barack Hussein. We also know in Barack's own words in his books about his youth that his adopted father, Lolo Soetoro, was an Indonesian citizen. Lolo adopted Barack Hussein, renamed him Barry, and made Barry a Muslim Indonesian citizen. On Barack's elementary school papers, Barry Soetoro, Barack Hussein, is listed as an Indonesian citizen and a Muslim with a signature of certification by his stepfather.

Many people are making a big deal about this new COLB being a forgery ... and maybe it is ... but if we accept what is says ... in that his father was Obama, Sr who was a Kenyan citizen ... then we need to concentrate on the real issues: did Barack Hussein ever use foreign citizenship to attend college or secure a passport as an adult? If he did, then he is not qualified to be president according to 8 USC 1481.

But will anyone pursue this now that the media has allowed Obama to frame this about where he was born rather than his dual citizenship? Certainly not the RINOs in Congress. They can't even man up enough to get any real cuts to government spending, so how can we ever expect them to grow enough balls to enforce our Constitution about the citizenship of the President?

So who will pursue the truth?

Why did Obama spend multi millions of dollars in legal fees to seal his college documents and his passports and his birth certificate? What is on them? Did he use foreign citizenship as an adult?

Sincerely,
Michael Master

Did Donald Trump deliberately distract America from the citizenship issue? Maybe. If he runs for president as an independent, then he definitely did. Anyone who runs for president as an independent is doing it just to split the Republican vote so Obama gets re-elected.

So what is the morality of radicals and community organizers? Read these words of Saul Alinsky again: " Does this particular end justify this particular means?" Any means is fair game to the radical, the community organizer, if it is justified by the end result.

Compromise

Saul Alinsky: "If you start with nothing, demand 100%, then compromise for 30%, you're 30% ahead."

Compromise is the key to the strategy of the community organizer. If position A is the starting point and position C is the desired position of the radical, then any movement towards position C is a win for the radical. The radical asks for everything and then falls back to some point (B) that is between the starting point and the end point.

When the social security system was first proposed during the presidency of Franklin Delano Roosevelt, the starting position was that there was no Social Security. So any amount of social security was more than what was the starting position. To get the legislation passed, Roosevelt agreed to impose limits on it. Contributions could not exceed more than one percent of the pay of the worker, and the contributions had to be used for retirement benefits for the worker who made the contributions. That was the compromise. That got the government foot in the door.

Since then, the federal government used a little noticed line in the legislation to use the Social Security Trust Fund for things other than payments to the contributor. The government raided the fund. LBJ and the Democratic Congresses of the 1960s were the first to raid it. They used it to finance the Great Society since most other funds were being used by LBJ for his Vietnam War. That little act of theft has now been duplicated by almost every administration since LBJ.

In reaction to that, the amount of contribution by employees has been increased to almost 7 percent. That increase of seven times has not saved the program because the government continues to raid it for other programs. The Social Security System morphed from an annuity program for the individual worker to a ponzi scheme where the current generation of workers pays the retirement benefits for the current retirees. When there are fewer people paying into the ponzi scheme than those who are taking out of it, then it falls apart. And since the baby boomers did not have enough children to replace themselves, the decreasing number of workers per retirees must pay more into the fund or it will operate at a deficit. Therefore, the Social Security Trust fund is close to insolvent today and the solution proposed by the government is to cut back on the benefits to retirees. The Social Security program became just another tax on people to finance other government programs.

Compromise. The government used compromise to get the American public to accept this new Social Security tax, and then government used those funds for something other than the intention. It then also incrementally increased the tax to where it wanted it originally. Compromises along the way allowed it to happen.

How many other things have been implemented by compromise and then "changed" to what was originally desired?

Abortion changed from only being allowed in the first trimester and only with the consent of parents, to abortion on demand for any woman who wants it at any time. Sales taxes increased from an original amount of 1 percent to an average of 6 percent. Sales taxes in some areas are as high as 10 percent. Property taxes increased 500 percent from a ¼ percent of the value of the house to an average of 1.25 percent. Gay equality for jobs changed to gay hate crime laws as a protected class. No prayer in schools expanded to the elimination of the impact of God and religion from history books, and historic speeches. This list goes on and on.

So what compromises are in the healthcare "insurance" legislation of 2010 of which Americans have no knowledge? What will healthcare insurance actually be in the future? What is being proposed as the compromise for environmental legislation that will eventually lead to everything that the liberals want? What compromises are unions getting that allow them to use Card Check that will allow them to be even more monopolistic?

Compromise is the secret weapon of the liberals. Compromise has been used to incrementally erode the freedoms of Americans. Compromise has been used by politicians to grow government (federal and local) into an abusive monster.

This chart represents the strategy of compromise. If position A is the starting position and position C is the desired liberal position, then liberals will ask for C and settle for B. Once B is achieved, then liberals will ask for C again at a later time and only settle for a compromise that moves closer to C until eventually they achieve the entire Liberal Position.

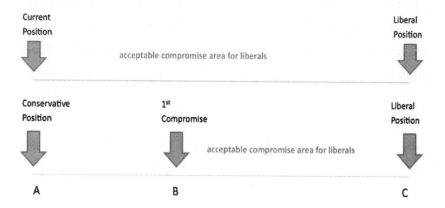

The teachers' strike in Wisconsin of February 2011 posed a most interesting situation. Facing a deficit in Wisconsin that would force the state into bankruptcy, the newly elected Republican legislature and governor proposed either laying off 5,000 teachers or cutting their government paid benefits. In addition, the Wisconsin legislature proposed becoming a "right to work" state which would in effect eliminate the labor controlled monopoly held by the unions. It is interesting to note that the states without this deficit problem are generally "right to work" states while the ones with deficit problems are union controlled states.

Wisconsin could have claimed bankruptcy and then eliminated all contracts, but instead chose a participative legislative approach. The teachers went on strike (which was illegal under their contract). President Obama stated his support for the unions and Democratic legislators fled the state so a quorum was not available for any legislation.

The teachers claimed that collective bargaining was their right. Those were the same teachers who are teaching our children. Those were the same teachers who are providing the worst education in math and science of any industrialized country at a cost per student that is the highest of any country in the world.

What in the state constitution or the U.S. Constitution says that collective bargaining is a right? Nothing. It is a privilege. It is the result of the contract between the government and the union. It is result of legislation as representation of the voters. It is certainly not a right. But that is what is claimed by these very teachers who are teaching our children. They failed at their jobs and then wanted to be rewarded for their failures.

First, why was the president of the United States interjecting himself into a state issue? Next, where was the media on all of this? They claim that collective bargaining is a right. And why? The answers are obvious—unions. They control Obama and they have a huge impact on entertainment and the media.

An obvious no-win situation was created by the Democrats, media, Obama, and teachers so that any compromise by Republicans would keep the legislature from doing the will of the electorate that just elected them—to reduce government costs and create a competitive situation by implementing "right to work."

The only compromise that was acceptable to those liberals was one that allowed them to continue the very practices that caused the financial problems. No compromise was acceptable that would take away any of their collective bargaining power or their labor monopoly.

Compromise. The tool of liberals. A little of this and a little of that—until they have everything that they want.

Conservatives could learn something from these liberals. Compromise is only good if it moves the ball in the direction that you want it to move.

Polarization (Demonize)

Saul Alinsky: "Men will act only when they are convinced that their cause is 100% on the side of the angels and that the opposition is 100% on the side of the devil."

Along with the rule of polarization is the tactic of demonizing the opposition.

The USA did not enter into WWII until 1941 when the Japanese attacked Pearl Harbor. The USA declared war not only on Japan, but then also declared war on Germany and Italy. Germany and Italy did not attack the USA. Prior to then, the American people did not yet see enough evil in the Nazis to declare war on Germany and Italy. FDR used the attack on Pearl Harbor to wrap Japan, Germany, and Italy into an evil Axis power and then asked Congress to declare war on all of them. FDR demonized Germany. He polarized America against Germany. Polarization worked.

Today, the media likes to point out how the electorate in the USA is polarized. It points out how the government is gridlocked because of this polarization. Oh, so true. But is that a bad thing if it slows down the actions of the government? Maybe not.

How did the gridlock happen? Because liberals have been painting a picture that the Haves are greedy and selfish. Liberals have caused envy in the Have-Nots to deliberately divide

America into the Haves and Have-Nots. There is no common ground between those who are Have-Nots and those who Have if the Have-Nots believe that the Haves are not deserving of what they have.

That is class warfare.

The community organizers, the radicals, the liberals have done an outstanding job of making the Have-Nots believe that all of the Haves gained their wealth by unethical means. They have done a good job of convincing the Have-Nots that the Haves are 100 percent on the side of the devil and that the Have-Nots deserve for the government to take some of the wealth of the Haves to give it to the Have-Nots. That is government- sanctioned theft.

The liberals couch this theft in terms like "social justice" and "redistribution of the wealth" and "reparations."

The teachers strike in Wisconsin in February 2011 showed how the liberals implemented this strategy as they referred to the Republican governor as Hitler—how they referred to the Republican legislature as evil people who were harming their rights. And the mainstream media allowed them to do it without any reference to those states who already eliminated collective bargaining like Virginia and most southern states. The mainstream media never mentioned that states with 'right to work" laws have budget surpluses rather than deficits like in Wisconsin.

What is most interesting is that the leaders of the Have-Nots like Nancy Pelosi, Charlie Rangel, Harry Reid, Christ Dodd, and John Kerry are some of the wealthiest in government. They gained enough wealth to become part of the Haves by organizing the Have-Nots. And the Have-Nots are so blind by envy of the Haves that they don't even see that their leaders are part of the Haves.

As the economy turned down in 2008, liberals blamed all of it on George W. Bush. Entertainers and media demonized him as the worst president ever, and constantly repeated the mantra that "It's all Bush's fault." Because of their relentless attacks, Bush's approval rating fell to less than 35 percent by the time he left office in January, 2009. But the facts said something else.

Jack Tymann, a friend and author for Red State, sent me this observation in an email on November 30, 2010:

January 3, 2007 was the day the Democrats took over the US House of Representatives and the US Senate at the start of the 110th Congress. This marked the first time that the Democratic Party controlled a majority in both chambers since the end of the 103rd Congress in 1995.

For those, the day the Democrats took over the Senate and the Congress, who are listening to the fallacy that everything today is "Bush's Fault," think about this:

- *On January 3rd, 2007 The DOW Jones closed at 12,621.77*
- *The GDP for the previous quarter grew at 3.5%*
- *The unemployment rate was 4.6%*
- *The US deficit was below historic norms as a % of GDP*
- *The USA, based on George W. Bush's economic policies, had just SET A RECORD of 52 STRAIGHT MONTHS of JOB CREATION!*

Then on January 3rd, 2007 Barney Frank (Democrat) took over the House Financial Services Committee and Chris Dodd (Democrat) took over the Senate Banking Committee.

15 months later we experienced a meltdown of US BANKING AND FINANCIAL SERVICES!!!

PS: from 2001 through 2008, George W Bush asked Congress 17 times to increase regulations on Fannie & Freddie - stating current policies with regard to both were financially risky for the US economy.

PPS: Republicans have controlled the Senate for all the increases to employment over the last 18 years (23 million new jobs). Democrats have controlled the Senate for all the decreases to employment over the last 18 years. Democrats have controlled the entire Congress for the last 4 years (loss of 7 million jobs).

Bush was demonized successfully by the liberals while the real culprits were the Democrats in Congress.

In 2009, the Tea Parties started. They were grass roots organizations of average Americans all across the USA. The first reaction to them by liberals was to refer to the Tea Party people as racists. Because Tea Party people were against any additional government and any additional taxes, the liberals claimed that Tea Party people must be racists because the ones who would be hurt the most by reducing government programs are minorities—blacks.

The term "racist" is a lightening rod in America. Liberals tried to demonize Tea Party people by calling them racists. When that didn't work, the liberals, especially the media, used the tragedy in Arizona in January 2011 to blame the deaths of the 6 people on the Tea Parties and conservative radio personalities.

Even though the facts proved that the shooter was deranged and that the Tea Parties had no influence on the shooter, the liberal media accomplished its objective of demonizing the Tea Parties. After Obama incited the Have-Nots for 3 years, the media allowed him to give a speech in Arizona that painted himself as the peace-maker.

How many years did the liberals continue the mantra that George W. Bush was the worst president ever? They burned him in effigy. They called him names and painted mustaches on his pictures to make him look like Hitler. This was part of the strategy to demonize him. They disparaged Bush daily to paint Bush as 100 percent on the team of the devil.

Then in 2008, the liberals actually presented Obama as "the one." They implied that he was the Messiah—100 percent with the angels—and ran him against the misrepresentation that McCain was just a clone of Bush—a clone of the devil.

Demonize Bush, paint McCain as another Bush, and then present Obama as the Messiah. It was a strategy right out of *Rules for Radicals.*

Obama went so far as to say, "We are the ones that we have been waiting for." Oh, how Jesus Christ must be cringing.

Liberal journalists like Chris Matthews were true apostles of Obama when Matthews referred to a thrill running up his leg as Obama gave a speech or when he accused Sarah Palin and the Tea Parties for motivating the Arizona shooter. That was the same Matthews who slammed McCain for picking Palin as a running mate because she did not have enough experience. In reality, Palin had more executive experience running for Vice President than what Obama had running for President. Matthews demonized McCain through Palin and canonized Obama.

None of those journalists who supported Obama have reviewed Obama's record against his promises. None of them have analyzed his misrepresentations. They continue to protect him because Obama really is their Messiah.

Liberals are doing exactly what Alinsky instructed radicals to do. He told them to demonize the opposition and then elevate the liberal leaders to sainthood. He told them to polarize the electorate. Deliberately. And that is exactly what they do.

Incite Discontent

Saul Alinsky: "In the beginning the organizer's first job is to create issues or problems."

The original community organizers singled out the school systems. They deliberately went into lower income school districts and convinced the people that their children were getting less of an education because they did not receive as much money for their schools as did the schools in the wealthier neighborhoods.

Because of the actions of the community organizers, children were bussed from far away neighborhoods and schools, and schools located in low-income neighborhoods received tons of money from the federal and local governments. The squeaky wheel got the oil. Study after study shows that bussing harmed students. Students spent too much time in transit.

Study after study also shows that there is no correlation between money spent per student and the academic achievement of students. The key variables to scholastic success are whether a child is raised by one parent or two and the amount of help parents provide in the education of their children.

Yet, the community organizer needed a reason for existence, so the school system became an easy target. The community organizer created discontent in the local people about their school system through envy of the schools in the wealthier neighborhoods. If the community organizer had been interested in children getting a better education, then he/she would have demanded that two parents raise the children and that those parents take active roles in educating their children. Instead, the community organizer used envy towards wealthy people to cause discontent. And in the process, the community organizer gained power.

Envy, coveting, is the number one tool of the community organizer. Class warfare. Race warfare. Gender warfare. They are all based on a strategy of creating envy. In the 2008 elections, Chris Matthews stated that the new-found political tool was envy. Democrats used envy and coveting to incite discontent among women vs. men, blacks vs. whites, Hispanics vs. law enforcement, low-income persons vs. highly paid people. It came in multiple shades of envy like healthcare for everyone and taxes on hedge fund managers and equal pay for women based on job category without regard for experience or skill level. But it was the use of envy, jealousy and coveting that incited the Have-Nots with discontent.

Create Mass Organizations
Saul Alinsky: "Organize the world."

Alinsky cites many objectives of John L. Lewis, one of the early leaders of the CIO union in the United States. He restates the words of Lewis to "organize the world." It is the ultimate goal of these liberal radicals to organize the world into one union, one united organization, one world order; and that process of organizing will provide the organizing leaders power over that world organization.

Alinsky banks on the fact that most conservatives see themselves as individuals. As such, conservatives are helpless against large organizations. Where the conservative says that the family is the most important unit in society, the liberal will say, "It takes a village…"

As stated in the *Art of War*, the largest army will win the war. So liberals are determined to have the largest army through unions … organizing.

And what are those unions? Teachers and public employees are now the largest union groups in support of the liberal agendas in the USA. And they teach our children with union bias and they determine government regulations with union bias.

Use Their Own Words Against Them. Then Ridicule, Ridicule, Ridicule

> Saul Ainsky: "*Make the enemy live up to their own book of rules.*" "*Ridicule is a man's most potent weapon.*" "*Maintain a constant pressure upon the opposition.*"

Alinsky quotes Jesus Christ from Luke 11:23: "He that is not with me is against me." Alinsky was a Jew. He used the words of Jesus Christ to justify his instructions to polarize groups into those who agree with the organizers and those who don't. He used these words of the Christian Bible to justify his instructions to demonize the opposition. He used the words of Christians against them.

Alinsky continues, "The one thing that is unforgivable and that is certain to get him to react is to laugh at him. This causes an irrational anger."

Now look at the actions of liberals for the last fifty years. Congressman Foley made phone calls that were sexually inappropriate. Liberals attacked him unmercifully. They laughed at those Republicans who would not condemn him. They called them hypocrites.

Now compare that to how liberals treated Bill Clinton when he committed perjury. First, the liberals claimed that the perjury wasn't important because it was about sex. Then when the sex issue was raised, they said that they didn't care. Not even Hillary Clinton cared. Liberals forced conservatives to condemn Foley because of conservative core values but had no care about the values themselves.

This has continually been the tactic of liberals about race, about bias, about bigotry, about Christian charity, about military security, about government spending—about everything.

Think to yourself how the liberals treated Bush about the economy in 2000. They blamed everything about it on Bush, even though the dotcom build up happened under Clinton. They blamed the $400 billion deficit on Bush, even though the Senate was controlled by Democrats. The economy fell apart under the Democrat Congress of 2007, they spent the USA into a $2 trillion deficit, refused to create a government budget, and let unemployment grow to 10 percent without ever accepting any responsibility.

How could they do that? Because they never said that they would not use deficits or that they would use budgets. They criticized Bush only because he was against deficits. So they used his words against him, even though they did not adhere to it themselves.

Conflict

Saul Alinsky: "All new ideas arise from conflict."

Alinksy is clear in his instructions. He instructs the community organizers to create conflict and use it to unite those that the organizer wants to organize. He uses an example of how he focused on a landlord for rent controls. Even though the landlord was willing to recognize rent controls, Alinsky ignored it. Instead, he created conflict with the landlord to unite the renters in the project.

He cites another example of how a government employee granted his wishes, but how he continued to holler and shout at the government employee to gain leadership of a group of people.

Alinsky takes conflict one more step. He states that most people do not like conflict. So to win concessions, he deliberately used conflict as a method of pain to get the opposition to negotiate and/or capitulate.

It is obvious that liberals use conflict to organize and to gain concessions ... while all the time blaming the conflict on the opposition. Bill Clinton did just that with the shutdown of the government when he was president. He caused a conflict with the Republican controlled Congress, which delayed the appropriation of funds. He then blamed it on Congress and took no responsibility for any of the conflict. Congress looked bad to the public. Clinton looked good. And Clinton got what he wanted from the Republican Congress.

Communication

> Saul Alinsky: "One can lack any of the qualities of an organizer—with one exception—that exception is the art of communication.... Communication with others takes place when they understand what you're trying to get across to them."

Alinksy does not include listening or understanding the other point of view as part of communication, other than to use information about the audience to sell the organizer's agenda. He continues by instructing radicals to use shocking, rude, and offensive language. He tells stories about how he used sexual swear words and other profanity to gain attention and demonize the opposition. Rahm Emmanuel used this very tactic in persuading hold-outs to vote for Obamacare. Obama used raw language and flipped his middle finger when discussing McCain during the 2008 election cycle. He incited conflict with these words, "If they bring a knife, then we will bring a gun." Alinksy states that the reason to understand the other person's life is to use that information to persuade that person to the radical's point of view.

The election of 2010 brought the most devastating losses to Democrats in local and federal governments since the great depression. While every poll suggested that the losses were because Americans did not agree with the Obama agenda, Obama personally stated that the losses were due to his inability to communicate his programs effectively. He honestly believed that he did not do a good enough job of "trying to get (his programs) across to them."

Obama did not entertain for a minute that America did not agree with him even after a full understanding of his programs. That is just not acceptable to a community organizer. Instead, the liberally controlled media has Obama on TV in some way every day to help Obama get his points "communicated."

To summarize the *Rules for Radicals* as presented by Saul Alinsky:

> *Liberals are at war with conservatives. As he spoke to Hispanics about conservatives and Republicans, Barack Hussein Obama stated just before the November 2010 elections that they (Hispanic Democrats) needed to "punish the enemy."*
>
> *The enemy? Obama sees Americans who are conservatives as the "enemy."*

Obama then used race-baiting rhetoric and said that conservatives could come along for the ride with liberals, but that conservatives would have to "ride in the back."

Is that a reference to riding in the back of the bus? Was it meant to incite race anger?

Michael Ledeen, in his book *Accomplice to Evil,* cites example after example of how good people in the world refused to accept the fact that others are evil even when the facts were placed right in front of them.

Hitler was clear about what he wanted to do if elected, but the western world listened to his words with filters that kept them from accepting the literal meaning of his words. There are still many people in the world today who reject the facts about Nazi atrocities, even with the overwhelming amount of pictures, witnesses, and other evidence.

Look how American universities invite evil leaders to address the students and then they shun those who have political beliefs that offend them. Look at how the UN continues to appease the leadership in Iran and North Korea even after their aggressive actions with nuclear weapons, and actions against their neighbors. Look at how Notre Dame University and Georgetown University covered Christian pictures and Crucifixes so they would not offend Obama on his visits to their campuses, but neither one questioned Obama's claim to be a Christian. Look at how the media in the U.S. has overlooked how Obama omitted the word "creator" three times in a row in September and October of 2010 as he quoted from the Declaration of Independence. Look at how moderates continue to ignore the literal words in the Koran that state it is the duty of Muslims to kill or enslave non-believers, and to lie to non-believers about their Muslim beliefs and motivations.

How many Americans still ignore the facts that Obama was part of ACORN and that he sealed the documents about his college education, his passports, and his long form birth certificate while claiming to be transparent? And how many Americans still ignore that Obama had close relationships with Bill Ayres, Tony Rezko, and Reverend Wright, who all practice these techniques of Saul Alinsky?

Saul Alinsky wrote on how to seize power. His tactics have been used by liberal leaders, labor union leaders, and community organizers since the 1960s. As stated by the *Chicago Sun-Times*, the list includes Barack Hussein Obama and Hillary Clinton. But so many good Americans refuse to recognize the tactics as a war against America because Americans just want to see the good in others, especially minorities, even though liberal leaders, union leaders, and community organizers admit to using those tactics.

It is time for conservatives to understand that liberal leaders are at war with them. Liberal leaders cannot be trusted. Their intentions in negotiations cannot be trusted.

In the very first chapter of *Rules for Radicals*, "The Purpose," Alinsky used a quote from the Old Testament, Job 7:1, which states: "The life of man upon earth is warfare."

Liberals have been at war with conservatives for the last fifty years. While conservatives have compromised with liberals in good faith, liberals have negotiated with conservatives in bad faith. The only objective of liberal leaders is to gain power for themselves. And they will use any or all of these tactics to do it:

- Propose change.
- Use any means as long as it is justified by the end.
- Compromise until everything is achieved.
- Polarize (Demonize).
- Incite Discontent.
- Create Mass Organizations.
- Use Their Own Words Against Them. Then ridicule, ridicule, ridicule.
- Cause conflict.
- Communicate.

When are good, God fearing Americans going to accept the fact that liberal leaders have been at war with American conservatives? That their internal "enemies" are more important to the liberal leadership than are the external enemies to America? And that those liberal leaders have been dividing America, manipulating Americans, for their own political gains?

As Saul Alinsky instructed, liberal leaders have been manipulating the Have-Nots and the Want-Mores in America to seize power for themselves.

They will use any means–ethical, unethical, legal, and illegal–as long as it is justified by the end results, and that includes Obama, Clinton, Reid, Pelosi, et al.

Chapter 2
America Today

Look around you. The results of Alinsky and liberals are everywhere.

Liberals offer change to the "Have-Nots" just as Saul Alinsky instructed them to do. Change. Any change. This might be so, but will change necessarily bring about anything that has lasting positive benefits for America?

A good friend, Sue Sarkis, sent me this story about change:

There's an old sea story about a ship's Captain who told the first mate that his men smelled bad. The Captain suggested perhaps it would help if the sailors would change underwear occasionally. The first mate responded, "Aye, aye sir, I'll see to it immediately!" The first mate went straight to the sailors berth deck and announced, "The Captain thinks you guys smell bad and wants you to change your underwear." He continued, "Leo, you change with Jerry. Tony, you change with Bert and Bob, you change with Ed."

THE MORAL OF THE STORY: Someone may come along and promise "Change," but don't count on things smelling any better.

The promises of liberal leaders include a clear statement of redistribution of wealth as part of their promise of change. That redistribution does not create any additional wealth in the economy. It lacks the touch of what entrepreneurs call "wealth creation." Wealth redistribution simply takes from some and gives it to others. That is theft. It is a retail mentality of distributing revenue that does not account for "creation" of additional revenue. In the long run, this kind of change, redistribution, will only create as much benefit as the first mate telling the sailors to change their underwear with each other.

Global Warming Alarmists and the Link to Reducing the World Population

How can so many ignore the impacts of negative population growth of the intrinsic population of the United States? How can so many ignore how our children—especially young women— are being brainwashed into thinking that children are a drain on their lives?

Please listen to me: Industrialized countries are losing in the world struggle between the Haves and Have-Nots. The industrialized countries are the Haves and they have lost population in the last forty years. All of the growth in industrialized counties is from immigration from the Have-Not nations. By attrition and immigration, the cultures of the Haves will be replaced within the next fifty years by the cultures of the Have-Nots. And why, you might ask? Because the New World Order wants to reduce the world population. To do that, they must neutralize the Have nations so they can eventually exterminate people in the Have-Not nations. They are neutralizing the industrialized nations by using the environment as an excuse for negative population growth—and the industrialized nations are following it like pigs to a slaughter.

The real objectives of those who are selling global warming to the rest of us are:

- To justify more government control, and
- To reduce the world population.

According to the *Globe and Mail* of Canada on December 5, 2010, Ted Turner told a global climate change convention in Cancun, Mexico that a one-child policy needs to be implemented throughout the world. That one-child policy would reduce the world population by half within 3 generations. And Mr. Turner thinks that will still be way too many people.

The Guardian of the United Kingdom posted this on December 3, 2010: "WikiLeaks cables reveal how US manipulated climate accord, Embassy dispatches show America used spying, threats and promises of aid to get support for Copenhagen accord."

WikiLeaks caused a major clash in America. The very people who screamed about secrecy in the Bush administration are the ones who condemned WikiLeaks for publishing documents about the abuses by government while the liberals have been in control. They show how the liberal government under Obama "cooked" the information on many things like foreign relations and climate information to justify their liberal World Order agenda.

Caucasian women have bought this environmental justification for not giving birth. Younger women, feminists, liberally educated women, place more importance on their careers than on being homemakers and mothers. The environment gives them one more excuse not to have children. The result is that the Caucasian population of the world has decreased from 24 percent of the total world population to 10 percent. Caucasians will soon be too small of a group to control the western civilizations. The U.S. will be the last to fall—but it will fall - from not enough births in the Caucasian population.

The following article by Jeff Poore is from the Business and Media Institute. An anonymous writer named "Conservative Coulter Fan" commented on the following on October 15, 2010:

The use of birth control has been an issue debated by ethicists in the United States for over a century. Until now, it's been a moral issue, and few mainstream voices ever advocated the use of birth control for environmental reasons.

On Scientific American's website, an Oct. 11 article by David Biello argues that if we were able to lower the growth of the world's population, the amount of carbon that is expected to be emitted into the atmosphere would significantly diminish. He cited a study from the U.S. National Center for Atmospheric Research that explained demographic ties to the alleged threats of global warming.

"An additional 150 people join the ranks of humanity every minute, a pace that could lead our numbers to reach nine billion by 2050," Biello wrote. "Changing that peak population number alone could save at least 1.4 billion metric tons of carbon from entering the atmosphere each year by 2050, according to a new analysis – the equivalent of cutting more than 10 percent of fossil fuel burning per year...."

"Ultimately, family planning alone—such as the use of condoms and other reproductive health services—in parts

of the world with growing populations, including the U.S.,
could restrain population growth significantly, this analysis
finds," Biello wrote. "It would appear that we're trying, thanks
primarily to ongoing efforts to enable women to take control of
their own lives through education and other methods..."

However in that paragraph, he linked another Scientific
American story from August 12, 2008 where he referenced
work by Stanford University scientists Paul Ehrlich and Robert
Pringle blaming humans for the extinction of thousands of
species. Their suggestion back then: Educate women about
"contraception and safe abortions."

That's why Ehrlich and Pringle call for educating women,
which has slowed or stopped population growth in the
developed countries of Europe. "Education and employment—
for women especially—along with **access to contraception**
and safe abortions are the most important components,"
they write. Adds Ehrlich: "The most basic response is to get
going on stopping population growth and starting a decline."

Although these arguments over the need to promote the use
of "birth control" for the environment's sake raise some ethical
questions, there is a belief more radical. Paul Watson, founder
and president of the Sea Shepherd Conservation Society in 2007
called for the world's population to drop below 1 billion, meaning
roughly 5.7 billion people would have to go away.

The lesser industrialized nations are not about to stop
breeding. So if only the industrialized nations are reducing their
populations, then who will be left to control the world in fifty
years? It will be a New World Order of elitists who will control the
socialized mass of Have-Nots from the lesser developed nations.

After the neutralization of the Haves in the industrialized nations through attrition, the New World Order will then become a totalitarian oligarchy that will implement its real objective of reducing the world population by more than three quarters (5.7 billion people). The cultures of the current industrialized nations will be gone. No one will stop the New World Order from implementing extermination and sterilization techniques to reduce the world population. But to gain that much control, the New World Order must eliminate the American culture as it has historically been the impediment to these types of tyrants. And to do that, they have used the liberals in America to convince the young women in America to not breed for reasons of their careers and the environment.

Federal and Local Governments

On May 4, 2010, *USA Today* carried a story, "Federal pay Ahead of Private Industry," that stated that government employees are paid 30 percent more than their counterparts in the same positions in the private sector. At first, most people did not believe it. Then it caused an uproar. But no politician has done anything to correct it.

How could this happen if government employees are meant to be servants to the private sector? How could this happen if government employees have less risk to their jobs? How could this happen if the private sector is the customer for government services? How could this happen if the private sector pays the taxes that are used to pay government expenses?

For like to like comparisons of job types, government employees are compensated much more than their counterparts in the private sector. That includes public educators who are compensated more than educators in the private sector. They are exempt from many of the government programs like the health "insurance" law (Obamacare). They have better pension plans. They have better medical insurance. They work shorter weeks and have more holidays.

The following is by Chris Edwards of the Cato Institute on August 24, 2009. Since then, several other organizations including *USA Today* on May 4, 2010 substantiated the data:

> *The Bureau of Economic Analysis has released its annual data on compensation levels by industry. The data show that the pay advantage enjoyed by federal civilian workers over private-sector workers continues to expand.*
>
> *The George W. Bush years were very lucrative for federal workers. In 2000, the average compensation (wages and benefits) of federal workers was 66 percent higher than the average compensation in the U.S. private sector. The new data show that average federal compensation is now more than double the average in the private sector.*
>
> *Figure 1 looks at average wages. In 2008, the average wage for 1.9 million federal civilian workers was $79,197, which compared to an average $50,028 for the nation's 108 million private sector workers (measured in full-time equivalents). The figure shows that the federal pay advantage (the gap between the lines) is steadily increasing.*

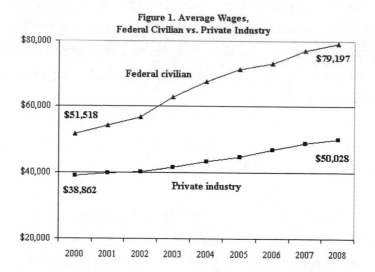

Figure 1. Average Wages,
Federal Civilian vs. Private Industry

Figure 2 shows that the federal advantage is even more pronounced when worker benefits are included. In 2008, federal worker compensation averaged a remarkable $119,982, which was more than double the private sector average of $59,909.

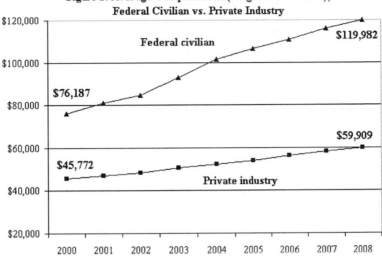

Figure 2. Average Compensation (Wages and Benefits), Federal Civilian vs. Private Industry

What is going on here? Members of Congress who have large numbers of federal workers in their districts relentlessly push for expanding federal worker compensation.

This happened during the years of George W. Bush and a Republican Congress (2002 to 2006) and a Democrat Congress (2000 to 2002 and 2006 through 2008). Republicans and Democrats are the same—they only disagree in public to make us in the private sector think that we have a choice between the parties. They are all government employees. When the unions of service employees and teachers are combined, they have the largest union in the USA. They vote for politicians who continue to provide them with more and more. Those promises are paid by the rest of the population, who pay the taxes to pay the government employees. Those government employees vote for those politicians who protect their positions, tenure, and income.

What employees in the private sector can elect bosses who will give them the most benefits and compensation? None. This could only happen in a democracy where government workers are allowed to vote for politicians who promise them the most benefits.

This did not happen overnight; it happened with each election cycle. Politicians made greater promises to teachers and other government employees during each election to gain votes. In the process, wages and benefits increased faster for government employees than for employees in the private sector. More employees were added to the rosters of the federal and local governments because more and more people want to work for the higher pay, security, and benefits of the governments. These government employees have become a huge political force with a huge appetite, so politicians in both parties make even more promises to gain their votes.

Look at this chart about the growth in the number of government employees:

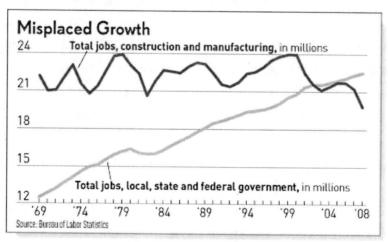

Misplaced Growth

24   **Total jobs, construction and manufacturing,** in millions

21

18

15

Total jobs, local, state and federal government, in millions

12

'69   '74   '79   '84   '89   '94   '99   '04   '08

Source: Bureau of Labor Statistics

Who paid for all of these new government employees (services and teachers)?

The employees in the private sector paid for them. Taxpayers paid for them. And taxpayers pay government employees more than what the same jobs get paid in the private sector.

And those government employees, including teachers, vote for those politicians who promise to take more of the money from the employees in the private sector, in order to give those government employees even higher pay and more benefits.

The USA Political System is Broken

Let me point out something. At a discussion at our Catholic church, we all agreed that one tenant of Christianity is charity—the voluntary act of helping others. If "we the people" could agree that we all need to give 10 percent of our earnings to help others, and then the government allowed a 10 percent credit to taxes for documented donations to organizations selected from a list provided by the government, then that would be charity. But instead, our government takes the money and gives it to those that it wants to have the money, and most of the time it is for political reasons. So that is theft.

Do you want your money to be spent on abortions? ACORN? Muslim studies? Uganda or Somalia? Or how about to GM to prop up labor unions—or for mandatory health "insurance" when all Americans have "healthcare" provided to them under other government programs?

Thomas Jefferson said: "To compel a man to subsidize with his taxes the propagation of ideas which he disbelieves and abhors is sinful and tyrannical." James Madison, who is sometimes referred to as the father of our Constitution, said: "Charity is no part of the legislative duty of the government."

The following is from my book, *Save America Now*:

As he left office, Dwight Eisenhower warned America about the military industrial complex. At that time, the industrialists were obtaining contracts to sell more and more stuff to the military. Those same industrialists would also make donations to the campaigns of politicians who would put more money into the budget of the military so it could award more contracts to those very industrialists who made the donations to the politicians.

This became a vicious cycle. It became a self-perpetuating machine.

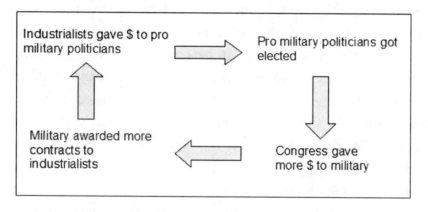

Well, today, the military industrial complex has been replaced by the social welfare and education complex.

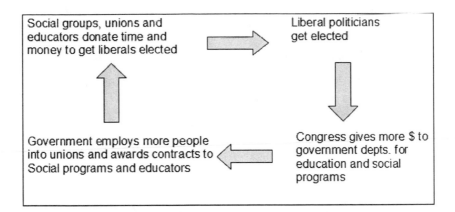

Social groups, unions and educators donate time and money to get liberals elected → Liberal politicians get elected

Government employs more people into unions and awards contracts to Social programs and educators ← Congress gives more $ to government depts. for education and social programs

Now let me add that John Adams warned America that when the government can take from some to give to others, democracy is lost. Politicians could buy votes with other people's money.

In America today, democracy is lost.

Obama received $20 million from insurance companies while McCain received $7 million. Pelosi, Reid, Dodd, and Schumer received more money from insurance companies than any other members of Congress. Obama received 10 times more money from lawyers than received by McCain and 80% of lawyers vote for Democrats. Obama, Pelosi, Reid, Dodd, and Schumer were the drivers for getting Obama-care passed through Congress. So is there really any wonder why the healthcare "insurance" bill was written in such a way that it helps insurance companies, and why it excludes any tort reform?

The political system in the US is broken. And these politicians will not fix it. The politicians are the reason why it is broken. Republicans and Democrats practice the same unethical tactics of bribery and theft through taxes; they just owe favors to different sets of people.

Neither party is motivated to fix the real root causes of our problems because the real problem is that our government is allowed to tax and spend with virtually no accountability. Politicians tax everyone to spend on those who help them gain power.

They have no motivation to curb spending. No motivation for term limits. No motivation to correct the imbedded root causes. "Change" to politicians means that they "change" who receives benefits from their legislation. That type of "change" does not correct problems.

The losers are conservatives who believe in the system because liberal Democrats and liberal Republicans are abusing conservatives all the time.

Immigration

America has laws about illegal immigration. Arizona passed laws that mirrored the national laws. The executive branch of the U.S. government decided to not enforce the laws given to it by the legislature, so it sued Arizona to stop it from enforcing those laws, claiming that only the executive branch of the federal government could enforce laws of immigration, and that a state had no jurisdiction in this matter. A federal judge agreed with the executive branch and stopped Arizona from enforcing those laws.

This raises so many questions that it is hard to know where to start.

First, it is important to note that the judge was a federal judge. Then note that the executive branch was not enforcing the laws that it was given from previous administrations and legislatures. So why didn't the judge challenge the executive branch as to what authority did the executive branch use to not enforce those laws?

America is in a sad state when politics are more important than what is right according to our Constitution. The Constitution was written to implement the mission stated in our Declaration of Independence. And the USA is wandering far from that mission statement as the USA turns its back on the illegal immigrant issue.

How can the executive branch unilaterally decide to not implement a law?

What do you think Mexico would do with illegal immigrants from south of its borders? Or what would Venezuela do? Or Iran? Or North Korea? So why does our executive branch get away without having to implement USA laws on illegal immigration?

As stated in *Save America Now,* this illegal immigrant issue stems from two things—first, the negative intrinsic growth to our population since the 70s; and second, the push for more liberal voters.

The negative intrinsic growth to our population in the 70s left the USA with too few low paid workers in the 90s and 2000s. The birth rate fell from 2.3 children per family to 1.3 at times. And 2.1 children per family is required just to maintain a population. Therefore, the percent of the population who were in their teens and 20s decreased in the 1990s and 2000s, which caused businesses to turn a blind eye to illegal immigrants; some businesses actually encouraged them, so there would be enough low cost workers for construction, restaurants, yard work, domestic work, etc. (Negative population growth in the 70s is also a major cause to the increased healthcare costs per person and to insolvency of the Social Security System).

What caused the negative population growth in the 70s? It was caused by the liberal push in our government for zero population growth. That push was used to justify funding of Planned Parenthood and taking abortion around the world to appease feminists. The USA, Western Europe, and Japan participated and are all suffering economically from that decision. Those countries who did not participate like Brazil, China, and India are still thriving.

The biggest harm is now felt in the housing market. Simply stated, there are fewer people between the ages of forty and fifty-five years old who are the most important consumers for the housing market. Those white people who would be in their middle ages today decreased because of low birth rates in the 70s and 80s, but this government will not say that because it will undermine the whole platform of liberals for the last forty years. Low interest rates, immigrants, and stimulus spending will not cure this problem of fewer white customers between forty and fifty five years old who purchase bigger houses and associated products like appliances and furniture.

Without immigrants and their offspring for the last forty years, the USA population today would be 200 million instead of 320 million. One third of a population from immigration is too much for a culture and an economy to assimilate, so now our culture and our economy are paying the price. First generation immigrants cannot replace the consumption of a decreasing intrinsic population.

A congressman who wishes to remain anonymous discussed this with me for an hour in his Washington office in the spring of 2010. He said that Congress was well aware of the problems caused by too low of a birth rate to Caucasians in the 70s and 80s. He went on to say that the federal government deliberately allowed immigration in large numbers in the 90s and early 2000s to compensate for those low birth rates. He said that Congress did not foresee the problems that would be caused by such a huge amount of immigration. They underestimated the effects on our health system, our schools, and our communities.

He said, "Congress did not foresee the problems of increased immigration." This is not only in the USA. It is throughout the industrialized world. England is feeling it. France is feeling it. All of Europe is feeling the pains of increased immigration to offset the impact of low birth rates to Caucasians. On October 17, 2010, the BBC posted an article about German Chancellor Angela Merkel, titled "Merkel says German multicultural society has failed." Merkel states: "(at) the beginning of the 60s our country called the foreign workers to come to Germany and now they live in our country." She added: "We kidded ourselves a while, we said: 'They won't stay, sometime they will be gone', but this isn't reality." "And of course, the approach [to build] a multicultural [society] and to live side-by-side and to enjoy each other... has failed, utterly failed."

Why did the Germans encourage immigrants to come to Germany for the last fifty years? Because they did not have enough younger, lower paid German employees to do the lesser jobs due to a negative birth rate 20 years before then. All of the industrialized nations had too low of intrinsic birth rates and all of them encouraged immigration to solve it. So all of them are paying a price economically and culturally because of it. And this is exactly what liberals and the New World Order want. It is the ultimate method to redistribute the wealth and to dilute the dominance of conservatives in traditional western cultures. The huge amount of immigration to industrialized countries from third world countries has been disastrous. Yahoo News posted this article on February 10, 2011:

PARIS (AFP) – French President Nicolas Sarkozy declared Thursday that multiculturalism had failed, joining a growing number of world leaders or ex-leaders who have condemned it.

"My answer is clearly yes, it is a failure," he said in a television interview when asked about the policy, which advocates that host societies welcome and foster distinct cultural and religious immigrant groups.

"Of course we must all respect differences, but we do not want... a society where communities coexist side by side.

"If you come to France, you accept to melt into a single community, which is the national community, and if you do not want to accept that, you cannot be welcome in France," the right-wing president said.

"The French national community cannot accept a change in its lifestyle, equality between men and women... freedom for little girls to go to school," he said.

"We have been too concerned about the identity of the person who was arriving and not enough about the identity of the country that was receiving him," Sarkozy said in the TFI channel show.

British Prime Minister David Cameron, German Chancellor Angela Merkel, Australia's ex-prime minister John Howard and Spanish ex-premier Jose Maria Aznar have also recently said multicultural policies have not successfully integrated immigrants.

The issue is not immigration. The issue is the volume of immigration. The issue is assimilation into the culture. And industrialized countries allowed huge amounts of immigration because their birth rates were so low. That huge volume hampered assimilation. Western Europe learned the hard way.

Countries like Russia and Japan pay people to have babies. What will it take for the USA to learn—quickly?

The push by liberals to enlist more voters has caused them to encourage more immigration. Liberals increased their ranks as the number of single women increased. Married people with children tend to be conservative. But since single women do not reproduce at a high enough level, liberals were left with no choice but to add to their ranks by allowing more and more immigrants into the USA and promising those immigrants more and more benefits to secure political support from the immigrants.

The profile of liberals has become one of single women (especially teachers), blacks, lawyers, Hispanic immigrants, Jews, and gays. Single women and gays do not reproduce, Jews have a low birth rate and are only 2 percent of the population, and Blacks are only 10 percent of the population, so the only alternatives for growth in the liberal portion of the USA are: (1) to allow more immigration; and (2) to brainwash the children of conservative families in our schools so they become liberals.

It does not make sense that liberals would push zero population growth and then push for more immigrants unless you understand the drive of liberals to justify abortion, the feminist agenda, and a state controlled benefit system.

The profiles of those who support liberal politicians have become people who want the government to take care of them and people who make money from government actions (government employees and lawyers/lobbyists)

This cannot sustain itself without taking money from conservatives to pay the bills for liberal promises. That is theft. It causes addiction to government – dependence. And it is the exact opposite of the intentions of our Declaration of

Independence and of the Tenth Amendment in the Bill of Rights.

States like Arizona are feeling the negative effects of unchecked illegal immigration. Gangs. Kidnappings. Drugs. Increased expenses for social services. Intimidation of children in public schools by immigrant gang members. Lower wages for citizens. Unemployment of citizens. Changing culture.

And so states like Arizona are in direct conflict with the direction of the liberals who now control the federal government. While we think that we change government with elections, liberals control the federal government through the permanent employees. The permanent government employees tend to be liberals, union members, single women, and minorities. Those employees make decisions every day that add more regulations, more socialization, more government, and more reliance on government in everything that they do.

A Dying Country

This cartoon was published in the *Chicago Tribune* in 1934. Look carefully at the plan of action in the lower left corner:

"Those who do not remember the past are doomed
to repeat it."

As discussed in *Save America Now*, Ravi Batra said in 1984
that a democracy would elect politicians who make the most
promises to the masses. Without strict controls on government—
like in our Constitution—those promises would eventually cause
socialism that would break the economy, which would cause
chaos, and lead to a dictatorship.

Liberals are fostering this cycle to pave the way for the
oligarchy of the New World Order. Our U.S. government is full of
these world order tyrants - the Fed, the World Bank, Democrats,
Republicans, Freddie Mac, Fannie Mae, and an industry full of
them with GE, who owned NBC; and George Soros, Ted Turner,
Bill Gates, and the Saudis who own a substantial portion of FOX.

Barack Hussein Obama is the front man in the USA for the world oligarchy. The courts are already in line. The military is being forced to change its loyalties from loyalty to "protect and defend the Constitution" to loyalty to the president. That will make the New World Order take-over hard to stop once the chaos from socialism happens.

Our children will be the ones to suffer. They and their children are being brainwashed. They are eagerly voting for socialism by the New World Order because it is disguised as helping those without healthcare, disguised as saving the environment, and disguised as stopping financial abuses.

Capitalism is being demonized in classrooms and entertainment. Our children and their children are being brainwashed into thinking that one world government would be a good thing.

So look closely at what is happening. The healthcare bill was about "insurance" and taxes, not healthcare. It adds 16,000 more IRS agents to collect more taxes. It increases the number of government union employees. The environmental bill was about taxes ... not the environment. The financial bill is about government control, not financial security. Bail outs are about helping the unions and members of Wall Street who support the liberals in government, not the economy. All of these bills are about giving more power to the government. And when do these politicians plan to replace our Social Security money that they used for other projects? Never. Instead, they propose cutting benefits and increasing taxes. They lie and they are corrupt.

Single women are the most susceptible. With the destruction of the family unit, single women vote for politicians who promise that the government will take care of them and their children. Single women and unions are electing liberals. They will end up suffering the most as those benefits that they expect from the government cannot be afforded. Single women are not "independent." They are dependent. They are addicted to the benefits that are provided by the government.

And this New World Order wants to dramatically reduce the world population. Read the health "insurance" bill. Look at the research being done by Gates. Read the words of Turner and read what was discussed at Bilderberg. They all believe that world problems like pollution and starvation and poverty are all caused by consumption by too many people in the world. And that only an oligarchy of elite can change it. The ultimate goal of the new world order is to reduce the world population substantially—by 70 to 90 percent.

The elite are trying to dismiss those who see this coming. They demean those who see the ties between liberal leaders to the New World Order as the real threat to democracy and freedom. The lesser elites have jumped on board. They disparage those who question Obama's citizenship and they attack those who question his violations to our Constitution. The lesser elites think they are included as part of the elite class. Lawyers and intellectuals are the worst. They will be the first to be canned by the New World Order. They helped Hitler get elected in 1932 and then got killed by him in 1938. Hitler promised socialism to get elected in 1932 and then gave them tyranny in 1938. And the lesser elites are all helping these New World Order tyrants manipulate what comes out of the media and what is taught in our schools today, just like they did for Hitler.

Batra wrote about this in 1984. He said that it was only a matter of time until Europe and the USA fell into the socialism trap, followed by chaos, which would be used to justify tyranny.

Dr. Jerome (Jerry) Corsi is a Ph.D in economics from Harvard.Five of his books have been on the top 10 list of the *New York Times*, including *ObamaNation* and *America for Sale*. Dr. Corsi shared these thoughts with me at a private lunch during a conference sponsored by *World Net Daily*:

> *The USA is not in a recession or a depression. The USA is suffering from a massive redistribution of wealth on a global scale that is being orchestrated by the New World Order and executed in the USA by Barack Hussein Obama and liberals … especially those in the media, government, and education. The financial pain in the USA will continue for quite some time until the standard of living of average Americans is reduced to the average of the rest of the world (by decreasing the standard in the USA and increasing the standard in third world countries)… or unless the American people stop participating in this communization of the world.*

The ultimate goal of the world elite is to have a dramatic reduction of people in the world, which will result in less consumption of world resources. To accomplish this, people need to be relocated from Third World countries to Western Europe and the USA and reproduction needs to be reduced to almost nothing. Why relocation? So those who reproduce learn to not do it in their new host countries, and so that the Haves are forced to take care of the Have-Nots.

Redistribution of the world population is the ultimate method for redistribution of wealth.

These World Order communists see two classes, an elite and a socialized mass. The losers in this will be the American people, families, and Christianity.

Socialized Healthcare "Insurance

It has been more than a year since Obamacare was signed into law. Insurance premiums are increasing and benefits are decreasing.

That is exactly the opposite of what was promised by Obama and the liberal Congress. Yes, insurance companies cannot refuse insurance to anyone for preconditions, but now we find that the rates they charge are not capped so those who have preconditions will pay exceedingly high rates for insurance. Yes, children must be covered until they are twenty six, but the insurance companies charge for it. Insurance companies gain new paying customers as extended dependents and from mandatory coverage. The Congressional Budget Office revised its estimate so now Obamacare will increase the deficit instead of decreasing it, as advertised at the start of 2010 (ha ha ha ha, what else is new?).

The new Republican led House of Representatives of 2011 investigated the details of Obamacare. It discovered that not only will Obamacare increase the deficit, but that there are many imbedded taxes in it. Without those taxes, Speaker of the House John Boehner said that that Obamacare would increase the deficit by one trillion dollars. The Democratic led House of 2010 and Obama did not tell America that so many taxes were imbedded in Obamacare and they claimed that Obamacare was deficit neutral. They lied.

So let me ask this question: Since so many in Congress used that original estimate of a decrease to the deficit to justify their votes for the "insurance" law, and since they claimed that there would be no additional taxes on Americans, will Congress redo the Congressional vote on it?

The new House of 2011 voted to repeal Obamacare. The repeal failed in the Senate. But now the new House refuses to defund Obamacare. So was that vote to repeal in the House purely an appeasement to conservatives?

It is estimated that millions of people will now lose their company provided insurance as many companies drop their insurance benefits. Medicare is scaling back in its benefits to elderly people, only 12 million of those 36 million people who could not get insurance will now have it because of Obamacare.

Of greatest concern is the fact that so many organizations are exempt from implementing Obamacare. Four states are exempt. That secured the votes from the representatives of those states. More than 1,300 companies and unions and government organizations are exempt.

This is the most corrupt government in the history of the USA.

No additional people will receive "healthcare." All those who gain "insurance" that did not have it already had access to free "healthcare" before this "insurance" legislation.

So was Obamacare worth it?

Yes, if you are an insurance company. No, if you are just an American citizen.

The October 1, 2010 *Kiplinger Letter* states that Republicans will not be able to reduce the impact of the healthcare insurance law because "The GOP cannot repeal the law as long as Obama is president." And "The health industry backs several big parts of the law..."

And why does the healthcare industry back this law? What do they have to gain from this "insurance" law? Why are so many unions and government employees exempt from it?

Let me add to the *Kiplinger Letter* that there are many Republicans who do not want to repeal it. They are liberals in conservative clothing. They also pander to special interest groups like insurance companies. Otherwise, they would be voting to defund it. They are RINOs (Republicans In Name Only).

Oh, special interest groups, special interest groups. Unions, lawyers, government employees, and insurance companies got everything that they wanted in this "insurance" legislation.

The following is from an op-ed that was written by me in February 2010. Things have not changed. Insurance companies and those people who are dependent on government benefits wanted this law, and liberals delivered it for them because it helped give more power to the government.

In the end, we the people got taken!

This is an op-ed by me that that appeared in Atlah Media Network before Obamacare was passed:

Title: "Insurance Companies are the Winners with Obamacare"
by Michael Master

As the insurance companies complain about the healthcare insurance bill, Democrats have written a bill that benefits those insurance companies. It mandates that all Americans must purchase insurance so it provides more young profitable customers to the insurance companies. It allows the government to reduce benefits so the insurance companies make more profit. It regulates fees paid to hospitals and doctors so the government acts as the negotiator for the insurance cartel.

More specifically, AARP will be a big winner if this bill passes. AARP is the giant insurer of the gap between Medicare coverage and medical costs. So as the gap increases from reduced payments, people will be forced to buy more gap coverage from AARP. Is there any wonder why AARP is promoting this?

… Obama is labeling opposition to ObamaCare as being against healthcare reform.

What if you want to reduce healthcare costs by reducing the insurance costs, taxes, and court costs of healthcare? Then you would not vote for the Obama package even though you want healthcare reform. Obama speaks with a forked tongue one more time as he paints this as a black or white issue, a race issue.

1. *According to statistics maintained by the Center for Responsive Politics, in the 2010 mid-term elections, Democrats have drawn 55% of insurance-related contributions, compared with 45% for Republicans.*

2. *The top three Senate recipients for insurance industry contributions —all Democrats—are Sens. Charles Schumer, D-N.Y., Chris Dodd, D-Conn., and Harry Reid, D-Nev., according to the center's research. And in the House, it's another trio of Democrats: Reps. Melissa Bean, D-Ill., Earl Pomeroy, D-N.D., and Barney Frank, D-Mass.*

3. *According to the Wall Street Journal of April 30, 2007, Nancy Pelosi and Steny Hoyer received a combined total of $2.4 million from the insurance companies.*

4. *The Washington Post of July 21, 2009 states, "Chairman Baucus (D-Mont.) has emerged as a leading recipient of Senate campaign contributions from the hospitals, insurers and other medical interest groups.… Health-related companies and their employees gave Baucus's political committees nearly $1.5 million in 2007 and 2008."*

5. *The Center for Responsive Politics shows that President Obama received a staggering $20,175,303 from the healthcare industry during the 2008 election cycle, nearly three times the amount of his presidential rival John McCain.*

Just like in the "Song of the South" when the rabbit says to the bear, "Don't throw me in that briar patch," the insurance companies are saying, "Don't pass this bill" … but they really want it. Otherwise, why would these Democrats be pushing it when they get so much money from insurance companies? …For this to be "healthcare" reform that benefits Americans, it needs tort reform (which lawyers oppose), it needs to eliminate insurance monopolies (which is missing from this bill), and it needs to provide "healthcare" to those who are economically deprived of healthcare (which was the original intent of reform).

This "insurance" legislation does none of that.

The Birth Rate

Liberals killed the economy when they legalized killing unborn babies.

On *Forbes on Fox* on January 30, 2010, the discussion turned to how population is affecting the USA economy. The panelists and Steve Forbes agreed that the USA needs more babies.

As documented in *Save America Now,* the number one variable affecting our economy today is the decision by our government from the late 1960s to 1985 to promote zero population growth. The number of births decreased in the USA. The birth rate fell from 2.3 children per family to 1.3 at times, while 2.1 children are required to maintain a population. That decreased birth rate has impacted everything from demand for products to healthcare costs to relaxed immigration laws, and to Social Security shortfalls.

As of 2008, the number of people between the ages of forty and fifty-five is decreasing as a percent of the total population. It is not a coincident that the economy took a dive in 2008. This age group has the highest impact on the economy. This age group has the highest income and it is consuming the most products. This age group lives in big houses which require lots of furniture. They buy additional cars. They pay the most taxes. Their children are teenagers and college students with big consumption. The number of people between forty and fifty-five decreased for the first time in forty years in 2008. So as this group decreased, then so did the economy. And this age group does not increase again until 2022.

The housing market is the perfect example. With fewer people between forty and fifty-five to purchase houses, there was more inventory than demand for houses. Therefore, the prices for houses decreased. As those prices decreased, many houses went "under water," which meant that more was owed on the mortgage for a house than the price that it could be sold. The result was foreclosures, lots of foreclosures; some voluntary and some involuntary. Those foreclosures caused more inventory of houses for sale, which in turn caused prices to fall even more. Prices fell more than fifty percent in some markets. The subprime loans that became full value loans were then unsustainable. The home equity loans that were obtained when the values were higher were then not worth the payments.

The reduction in people between forty and fifty-five is one of the items that is directly attributable to the crisis in the housing market, and all the ancillary industries like furniture and appliances. So, we all must ask, "Why didn't our government tell us about this?"

In contrast, the number of people over fifty-five is increasing, but they consume less real products. They consume more services like healthcare, which have very little multiplier effect on the economy as compared to consuming products. Their children left home. They downscaled their houses. They downscaled their product consumption. A person over fifty-five consumes ten times more healthcare than one under fifty-five. So those baby boom children of the 1940s and 1950s are increasing healthcare costs per capita as they age while they consume fewer real products without enough people between forty and fifty-five to offset them.

That decision to have fewer babies in the 1970s has caused healthcare costs to increase on average per person, caused demand for manufactured products to decrease, caused the demand for housing to decrease, and caused insurance companies to welcome Obamacare as a reason to not insure elderly people. The insurance companies want the government to pick up insurance for those over fifty-five.

And who convinced America to have fewer babies in the 1970s? Liberals. Liberals were looking for any reason to justify abortion throughout the world. They placed a woman's right to choose as more important than an unborn child's right to life. They claimed that the 3 billion people on earth at that time would consume the earth when the population reached 4 billion. They predicted starvation, war, and genocide at 4 billion.

Well, today, there are 7 billion people on the planet and none of the catastrophes forecasted by the liberals have happened. Those societies who decreased birth rates such as Western Europe, Japan, and the USA are now hurting economically. And those countries such as like Brazil, China, and India who ignored it are thriving.

Those liberals today are the very ones who now propose that our government step into the situation with more government. More government for bailouts. More government for regulating healthcare insurance costs. More government to stimulate the economy. More government for everything. They are using the crisis in the economy that they caused to justify more government.

Liberals not only support abortion, they encourage it. They teach our daughters that their careers are more important than motherhood. They support partial birth abortion and infanticide. Barack Hussein Obama specifically voted to allow infanticide and partial birth abortion while serving in the Illinois state legislature. Liberals want no restrictions on abortion of any kind while they promote more government intervention to correct the problems from zero population growth that a liberal government caused.

When Ronald Reagan was president, he complained that 15,000,000 abortions since *Roe v. Wade* had robbed America of its next generation of Americans. He was right. It is negatively affecting our economy today. Did anyone listen to him?

Since then, the most reliable estimates are that another 38,000,000 abortions occurred. So 53,000,000 abortions have occurred since Roe v. Wade. Those abortions and the lack of offspring from those murdered unborn children would account for more than 100,000,000 people. The 100,000,000 immigrants and offspring who grew the USA population (1/3 of the current total USA population) in the last 40 years would not have been needed if those 53,000,000 abortions had not happened. Those abortions have cost America its future and its culture and its economy.

That is karma. America is reaping what is sowed.

It is stupid to think that programs from those very liberals who caused zero population growth (actually it was negative population growth) are going to correct the problems to the economy and healthcare.

Government intervention caused the problem. More government intervention will not solve the problem.

We need to get back to having babies. We need to get back to "growing" America without government restrictions. Just think what this world will be in another fifty years if the third world countries continue to have five babies per woman and the industrialized countries continue to have less than one child per woman?

If our children do not listen to this, then their problems with the economy, with Social Security, with healthcare costs, with cultural changes in thirty more years will be even greater than those that we face today. But our children will not get this message as long as education and the media are controlled by liberals.

Peter Morici, professor of economics at the University of Maryland, was a guest on several financial TV shows in 2010, including MSNBC, CNBC, Fox Financial, and Fox News.

Professor Morici said that one of the root causes to our economic problems is: "That there is not enough demand for goods and therefore there is not enough consumption to create more jobs. And this cannot be cured by lower interest rates or by more investment money or by 'deals.'"

Why is Peter Morici one of the only other people to say this out loud?

Since the birth rate was so low in Western Europe, Japan, and the United States in the 1970s through 1985, there are not enough forty to fifty-five year old consumers to replace the decreasing consumption of the aging baby boom generation. And that affects everything. There is less demand for cars, housing, appliances, and furniture. The baby boom generation did not give birth to enough children to replace themselves as they aged.

On the telephone on September 3, 2010, Professor Morici told me that this current federal government knows the lack of demand is the root cause to the economic problems, but it refuses to do anything about it. This administration knows that bailouts, investments in corporations like GM, and stimulus projects do not solve the problem of decreased demand for products.

So why would this White House or Congress refuse to discuss this lack of demand for products? Why would they continue to spend tax-payer dollars on economic programs that they know will not help correct the problems caused by decreasing demand?

Let me say this in one word: *politics*.

The current government is using this economic crisis to take over industries like healthcare, force the U.S. into socialism, and justify open borders. It is using this crisis to steer money to its political friends like ACORN and George Soros and GE (MSNBC and NBC) and insurance companies. It is using this situation to help unions like the teachers' union and service workers without fixing the lack of consumption caused by negative population growth.

The government has been using the low birth rate to justify more immigration, which is a disaster for the intrinsic population.

If the government admits that there is too little demand because of the falling birth rate to Americans, then many of us are going to ask, "Why did the birth rate fall so much?"

The answer is going to be simple: Liberals in America, Western Europe, and Japan convinced the younger people to not have children. They did this in our schools, in the movies, on TV, and with the tax structure. Liberals emphasized abortion, contraceptives, an attitude of *Sex in the City,* and the glamour of being single. They convinced the young people in the industrialized world that careers are more important than having children, while the young people in developing countries continued to breed like bunnies. Liberals destroyed family values and the birth rate in the industrialized world.

If you doubt this, then sit in a college classroom or a high school classroom, watch TV, and go to the movies. What is being emphasized? Feminists, gays, and New World Order liberals are in control of the classrooms and entertainment. They brainwash our young.

In 2010, the birthrate for the white populations fell again in Western Europe and the USA to less than half of the two children per woman that is needed to support a steady state population. The white population of industrialized nations has fallen from 25 percent of the total population of the world to less than 10 percent in the last fifty years because white people are not breeding, while people in developing countries are breeding a lot, especially Muslims and Hispanics. The entire growth of the world population is from developing countries and immigrants from those developing countries.

The 2010 census of the USA is revealing many interesting facts. The *USA Today* of December 21, 2010 carried articles that pointed out that the birth rate for the last couple of years for women between 20 and 40 is at an extremely low point, and that growth to the population from 2000 to 2010, at 9.7 percent, is the lowest since the 1930s. That 9.7 percent is equivalent to roughly 26 million people. Legal and illegal immigration for those same ten years has been more than 50 million people. So that means the intrinsic population of the USA lost population again in those ten years by more than 10 percent of the population (25 million people). Blacks increased population and Hispanic Americans increased population, so that means that the white American population accounted for the entire 10 percent loss (25 million people) because they did not breed enough.

Caucasians made up more than 80 percent of the USA population in 1980. As stated in *USA Today*, the population of the U.S. will reach 400 million by 2050. Because of the low birth rate to Caucasians and the huge amount of immigration, at the current pace whites will be less than 50 percent of the population by 2050. All of the 100 million people growth between 2010 and 2050 will be from non-white citizens and immigrants. The white population will actually decrease.

Let me say this to those Caucasians who think that their careers and their *Sex in the City* life styles are more important than having children: If no children, then no future.

A society, a culture that does not have enough childbirth to replace itself is a dying society. The white people in America and Europe are not having enough children to replace themselves. So the white society, culture, is a dying society.

The *Art of War* says that those who have the largest army will win the war. Well, the white army is decreasing in the world to where it will soon be irrelevant.

No children, then no future!

Single White Women

Phyllis Schlafly, president of *Eagle Forum*, is an outspoken woman against the liberal feminists in America. She believes that the feminists have made women too dependent on government. And women are more enslaved because of it. At a fund-raiser on July 28, 2010, Schlafly stated:

> *Unmarried women, 70 percent of unmarried women, voted for Obama, and this is because when you kick your husband out, you've got to have big brother government to be your provider."* *She added that Obama is trying to boost welfare rolls to help with his reelection and to help Democrats.*

Democrats were outraged that Ms. Schlafly was pointing out something as obvious as that single women are looking to the government to replace the role of traditional husbands. Instead of debating the facts, liberals tried to paint her as anti-women, just like how they paint the opposition to Obama as racist. And, of course, the liberal media cartel disparaged her rather than discuss her theory.

In my book, *Save America Now*, the statistics about how more than 70 percent of single white women joined with 96 percent of Blacks, 80 percent of Jews, and 80 percent of gays to elect Barack Hussein Obama are indisputable. While white married women and white men voted overwhelmingly for McCain, single white women, especially less than 40 years old, voted more than 70 percent for Obama, and many of them convinced their parents to vote for Obama. Why were single white women so different than married white women or than white men? Family values are being destroyed by liberals. With it, they are destroying the security that comes with marriage—deliberately—as they push more dependence on government and decrease in independence of each American that is our heritage from our Declaration of Independence. So Democrats are presenting the government as the care-taker of single women and their families as the replacement for husbands. In the last election, Obama promised healthcare for everyone—not healthcare insurance—redistribution of wealth, closing a perceived pay gap between women and men—which is actually nonexistent when pays are compared for the same jobs at the same experience and performance levels—and more welfare benefits for single parents. So, of course, single women voted for Obama. They were bought. They want help at caring for themselves and their children. And so they embraced the socialism presented by Obama. Add the fact that teachers in the USA are 80 percent women and that they belong to the NEA or other unions, then it becomes obvious that the Democratic Party is pandering to the needs of single women to the detriment of the rest of America and our Constitution so that they can secure dollars and support from teachers who provide 25 percent of all monies contributed to Democrats.

Now here is the issue: Do "we the tax payers" of America want the changes that these liberal politicians are implementing to appease single women, Jews, gays, and Blacks? Do we want these fundamental changes to the values of America? Single parents. Socialism. Secularism. Children raised without a sense of traditional values.

Before you say that it doesn't matter, look at the results of where this has been tried. Look at Detroit and other big cities where more than 70 percent of children are born out of wedlock and where more than 70 percent of children are raised without a father. Look at the statistics about drugs, teenage pregnancy, crime, government insolvency, and illiteracy. In every case, when these statistics turned negative, they were preceded by a rise in the number of children raised by single parents.

Special Interests

Governments grow. It is the natural instinct for anything to grow—except for the current Caucasian population. The USA government has grown so large that it overshadows everything else in our economy and in our system of values. As shown in *Save America Now,* the collective impact of state, local, and federal governments is more than 40 percent of the USA economy. The combination of those collective governments takes more than half of pay of the average worker in the forms of taxes, fees, tolls, imbedded taxes, etc., to pay for those collective governments. Governments take more than half of the individual incomes of those people who work so they can tell us what to do in the guise of protecting us.

Who controls government? Special interest groups who are destroying the foundation of our nation. Who are those special interest groups? They include everything from insurance companies to horse breeders. They include associations who ban together and unions who claim to represent individuals. The only people who are not represented by special interest groups are those who act as individuals—citizens.

The largest special interest group in the U.S. today is the group made up of permanent government employees. This includes anyone who is employed by governments, which includes those who handle traffic tickets, those who aid Congressmen, those who are teachers, etc. As shown in *Save America Now,* permanent government employees now outnumber the employees in the combined total of the construction and manufacturing industries.

It is important to remember that Congress, judges, and the president are also government employees with the same thought process of the permanent government employees. Their task is to take more money and power from the private sector to provide more income and power to themselves. That is no different than the objective of Great Britain when our Founding Fathers wrote the Declaration of Independence in 1776. It is tyranny.

This current government is implementing a structure that is one of government elitists and their elitist friends (lobbyists, media, and educator intellectuals) who will preside over the socialized mass of the rest of us. The legislature, executive branch, and the courts have allowed this to happen in direct violation to their contract with "we the people." Many of them have encouraged the violation as payback for political debts.

The three branches of government are an incestuous group. They turn to each other for validation and verification. The legislature asks its own Congressional Budget Office (CBO) to verify the data it is using to justify its actions. The executive branch asks its own Office of Management and Budget (OMB) to verify the data and information that the executive branch uses to justify its actions. The OMB and the CBO look to the individual agencies for specific industry information. The agencies report to the president. The heads of the agencies are appointed by the president and ratified by the legislature. And the judges in the judicial branch who judge the legality of it all are selected by the president and ratified by Congress. They are all government employees. They are an incestuous group with allegiance to each other more than to "we the people." These people and their supporters are the liberal radicals in America. They are the enemies to America.

The check and balance on these groups is meant to be one of a three-sided teeter-totter where the three sides are the judicial branch, the legislative branch, and the executive branch. But if all three sides are of the same political persuasion—federal government versus states' rights or states versus individual rights, then who is checking on them? And if they are getting elected by the permanent government employees, then who is checking on the permanent employees?

The situation of the USA federal and local governments today is one that is of the government employees, by the government employees, for the government employees (including teachers, permanent government workers, and politicians) rather than of the people, by the people, for the people. This inbreeding between the legislative branch, the executive branch, the judicial branch, and the permanent government employees has caused this government to be the most corrupt government in the history of the US.

The Loss of Manufacturing

dweber2262@comcast.net   sent the following to me in an email in December 2010:

> The United States is rapidly becoming the very first "post-industrial" nation on the globe. All great economic empires eventually become fat and lazy and squander the great wealth that their forefathers have left them,

but the pace at which America is accomplishing this is absolutely amazing. It was America that was at the forefront of the industrial revolution. It was America that showed the world how to mass-produce everything from automobiles to televisions to airplanes. It was the great American manufacturing base that crushed Germany and Japan in World War II.

But now we are witnessing the deindustrialization of America. Tens of thousands of factories have left the United States in the past decade alone. Millions upon millions of manufacturing jobs have been lost in the same time period. The United States has become a nation that consumes everything in sight and yet produces increasingly little. Do you know what our biggest export is today? Waste paper. Yes, trash is the number one thing that we ship out to the rest of the world as we voraciously blow our money on whatever the rest of the world wants to sell to us. The United States has become bloated and spoiled and our economy is now just a shadow of what it once was. Once upon a time America could literally out produce the rest of the world combined.

Today that is no longer true, but Americans sure do consume more than anyone else in the world. If the deindustrialization of America continues at this current pace, what possible kind of a future are we going to be leaving to our children?

Any great nation throughout history has been great at making things. So if the United States continues to allow its manufacturing base to erode at a staggering pace, how in the world can the U.S. continue to consider itself to be a great nation? We have created the biggest debt bubble in the history of the world in an effort to maintain a very high standard of living, but the current state of affairs is not anywhere close to sustainable. Every single month America goes into more debt and every single month America gets poorer.

So what happens when the debt bubble pops?

The deindustrialization of the United States should be a top concern for every man, woman and child in the country. But sadly, most Americans do not have any idea what is going on around them.

For people like that, take this article and print it out and hand it to them. Perhaps what they will read below will shock them badly enough to awaken them from their slumber. The following are 19 facts about the deindustrialization of America that will blow your mind:

1. *The United States has lost approximately 42,400 factories since 2001. About 75 percent of those factories employed over 500 people when they were still in operation.*

2. *Dell Inc., one of America's largest manufacturers of computers, has announced plans to dramatically expand its operations in China with an investment of over $100 billion over the next decade.*

3. *Dell has announced that it will be closing its last large U.S. manufacturing facility in Winston-Salem, North Carolina in November. Approximately 900 jobs will be lost.*

4. *In 2008, 1.2 billion cell phones were sold worldwide. So how many of them were manufactured inside the United States? Zero.*

5. *According to a new study conducted by the Economic Policy Institute, if the U.S. trade deficit with China continues to increase*

at its current rate, the U.S. economy will lose over half a million jobs this year alone.

6. *As of the end of July, the U.S. trade deficit with China had risen 18 percent compared to the same time period a year ago.*

7. *The United States has lost a total of about 5.5 million manufacturing jobs since October 2000.*

8. *According to Tax Notes, between 1999 and 2008 employment at the foreign affiliates of U.S. parent companies increased an astounding 30 percent to 10.1 million. During that exact same time period, U.S. employment at American multinational corporations declined 8 percent to 21.1 million.*

9. *In 1959, manufacturing represented 28 percent of U.S. economic output. In 2008, it represented 11.5 percent.*

10. *Ford Motor Company recently announced the closure of a factory that produces the Ford Ranger in St. Paul, Minnesota. Approximately 750 good-paying middle class jobs are going to be lost because making Ford Rangers in Minnesota does not fit in with Ford's new "global" manufacturing strategy.*

11. *As of the end of 2009, less than 12 million Americans worked in manufacturing. The last time less than 12 million Americans were employed in manufacturing was in 1941.*

12. *In the United States today, consumption accounts for 70 percent of GDP. Of this 70 percent, over half is spent on services.*

13. *The United States has lost a whopping 32 percent of its manufacturing jobs since the year 2000.*

14. *In 2001, the United States ranked fourth in the world in per capita broadband Internet use. Today it ranks 15th.*

15. *Manufacturing employment in the U.S. computer industry is actually lower in 2010 than it was in 1975.*

16. *Printed circuit boards are used in tens of thousands of different*

products. Asia now produces 84 percent of them worldwide.

17. *The United States spends approximately $3.90 on Chinese goods for every $1 that the Chinese spend on goods from the United States.*

18. *One prominent economist is projecting that the Chinese economy will be three times larger than the U.S. economy by the year 2040.*

19. *The U.S. Census Bureau says that 43.6 million Americans are now living in poverty and according to them that is the highest number of poor Americans in the 51 years that records have been kept.*

So how many tens of thousands more factories do we need to lose before we do something about it? How many millions more Americans are going to become unemployed before we all admit that we have a very, very serious problem on our hands? How many more trillions of dollars are going to leave the country before we realize that we are losing wealth at a pace that is killing our economy? How many once great manufacturing cities are going to become rotting war zones like Detroit before we understand that we are committing national economic suicide?

The deindustrialization of America is a national crisis. It needs to be treated like one.

As pointed out in *Save America Now*, there are three major reasons for the loss of manufacturing in the USA:

- Unions have priced labor so high that costs for producing goods in the USA are more than 2 times the costs in Asia.
- The universities in the USA turn out only one quarter of

> the engineers and scientists per capita as are produced in Asia and Germany.

- The roll up of taxes in the manufacturing supply chain adds so much to the price of products that the USA products are not price-competitive.

Liberals increased the costs of manufacturing and reduced the engineering resources available to manufacturing companies, and then blamed corporations for outsourcing manufacturing. Now let me point out my opinion that the leaders of the World Order made a deal some time ago. That deal sets up geographic ownership of certain tasks. The West produces food. Western Europe manages the money. Asia manufactures products. And the Middle East provides the energy. Liberals think this is a good thing because it builds an interdependent world. This is in direct opposition to the "independence" established in our Declaration of Independence.

In my mind, this huge cartel has been manipulating the world for the last fifty years to get to this point. This plan also includes a huge migration of people from developing countries to industrialized countries until stabilization of the masses is reached, and population reduction can begin.

The U.S. could be independent, but continuously chooses to be more and more dependent on the rest of the world. An example of this was posted to our email group by Sue Sarkis on December 19, 2010, which is probably more common than not:

> *The country's largest manufacturer of sleeping bags says new competition from Bangladesh could force it out of business if the U.S. does not level the playing field.*

Exxel Outdoors Inc., which employs nearly 70 workers in its Alabama factory and makes about 2 million sleeping bags per year, has been pressing the Obama administration to lift an exemption that lets Bangladesh import sleeping bags into the country without paying a 9 percent tariff.

"You can't leave an American manufacturer at a competitive disadvantage with a foreign worker," Harry Kazazian, chief executive of the company, told FoxNews.com.

But that's apparently what the Obama administration has done, turning down the company's request in an initial ruling and forcing Exxel to submit another request.

The office of the U.S. Trade Representative, which is reviewing Exxel's request, told FoxNews.com that its review will conclude in the spring and that President Obama would have to sign off on any changes to the list of duty-free products – changes that would go into effect before July 1. "We take Exxel's concerns seriously," the office said in a statement.

Exxel is also seeking help from Congress.

Sen. Jeff Sessions , R-Ala., has tried to slap a tariff on Bangladesh sleeping bags but he has been unable to sway his fellow lawmakers to change the U.S. Generalized System of Preferences, or GSP, which determines which products third-world countries can import duty free....

Sleeping bag imports have been on the duty-free list since Czechoslovakia successfully lobbied for it in the early 1990s. But the country, which split soon afterward into the Czech Republic and Slovakia, never followed through with its plan to get into the sleeping bag business, leaving the loophole dormant until Bangladesh took advantage in recent years, an Exxel official told FoxNews.com.

The company says it has been able to compete with China because the communist regime isn't exempt from the tariff on its sleeping bag imports. But the company says in 2009 it began losing major orders from large U.S. retailers because of new sleeping bag operations in Bangladesh flooding the market with their imports.

Exxel says if its factory is forced to move offshore or close down, the economic ripple effect would hurt the company's U.S. vendors, such as suppliers of sewing thread, sleeping bag fill, packaging, as well as suppliers of trucking services and other factory supplies.

This story about Exxel shows the importance of the multiplier effect on the economy from the manufacturing supply chain. Government bailouts and spending on services and banking deals may help the stock market, but they cannot replace the effect of losing manufacturing on the economy as a whole. While stock prices and bond prices can be manipulated by money supply, jobs will not increase until manufacturing, oil, and the birth rate problems are fixed.

The government, liberals, and unions caused the exodus of manufacturing from the US. Taxes, education emphasis, and labor costs are at the heart of the issue. It is obvious that something is more important to the supposed leaders of America than American independence. Otherwise, the "leaders" would do what is necessary to really bring manufacturing back to America. They would force educators to emphasize engineering rather than liberal arts, they would reduce the roll up of taxes in the supply chain, and they would help companies reduce costs by regulating unions as monopolies.

Josh Frase is a contributor of information to a personal email exchange group. This is an edited email that he wrote to me:

Thanks very much for your article on why America is dying. Excuse the crudeness of my email, I have never been to college, I was homeschooled for my last three years of high school, and I have been working in the private sector from the time I was 15. For this reason my knowledge is very heavy on practical application experiences and very light on theoretical experiences, which are what motivate the bulk majority of commerce in today's American economy.

I think that one thing you are missing in your breakdown of the business cycle you articulated is the reason businesses dye in the legal stage. Laws are introduced to limit or remove errors. But the problem with this is it requires grace and mercy or overlooking error to perform research and development. The lack of America's ability to perform research and development due to the overwhelming number of laws here, I believe greatly reduces innovation....

So what do companies do? They go to other nations where the regulation is less severe on mistakes and the innovation takes place in those countries.

Getting from the legal side to the R and D side is very difficult in today's business environment. Most people in the upper positions where trained in colleges and universities where they studied theories. The problem with theories is that they are tested in a perfect world or in a lab where variables are greatly limited. When you get out in the real world and test those theories they often times fail because the amount of variables are greatly increased. Most who have gone through college have not ever had an opportunity to recognize this....

I thought I would throw this idea at you to contemplate. Again excuse the crudeness of my writing, I taught myself most of the English and writing skills I know.

Thanks again for your article and for your time,

Josh Frase

Government Run Education

The debates during the 2008 election cycle exposed the poor record of public education in the USA. Costs per student are among the highest in the world while achievement for math and science are at among the lowest. The union and government run educational system is going the same route as union controlled industry—higher pay and benefits with lower results.

In *Who Owns the Future?*, Pat Buchanan made the following comments on December 28, 2010:

Every three years, the Paris-based OECD holds its Programme for International Student Assessment (PISA) tests of the reading, math and science skills of 15-year-olds in developing and developed countries. Gurria was talking of the results of the 2009 tests.

Sixty-five nations competed. The Chinese swept the board. The schools of Shanghai-China finished first in math, reading and science. Hong Kong-China was third in math and science. Singapore, a city-state dominated by overseas Chinese, was second in math, fourth in science. Only Korea, Japan and Finland were in the hunt.

And the U.S.A.? America ranked 14th in reading, 17th in science and 25th in math, producing the familiar quack-quack. "This is an absolute wake-up call for America," said

Education Secretary Arne Duncan. "We have to face the brutal truth. We have to get much more serious about investment in education." But the "brutal truth" is that we invest more per pupil than any other country save Luxembourg, and we are broke....

We do not know how to close the gap in reading, science and math between Anglo and Asian students and black and Hispanic students. And from the PISA tests, neither does any other country on earth. The gap between the test scores of East Asian and European nations and those of Latin America and African nations mirrors the gap between Asian and white students in the U.S. and black and Hispanic students in the U.S. Which brings us to Bad Students, Not Bad Schools, a new book in which Dr. Robert Weissberg contends that U.S. educational experts deliberately "refuse to confront the obvious truth."

"America's educational woes reflect our demographic mix of students. Today's schools are filled with millions of youngsters, many of whom are Hispanic immigrants struggling with English plus millions of others of mediocre intellectual ability disdaining academic achievement."

In the public and parochial schools of the 1940s and 1950s, kids were pushed to the limits of their ability, then pushed harder. And when they stopped learning, they were pushed out the door. Writes Weissberg: "To be grossly politically incorrect, most of America's educational woes vanish if these indifferent, troublesome students left when they had absorbed as much as they were going to learn and were replaced by learning-hungry students from Korea, Japan, India, Russia, Africa and the Caribbean."

Weissberg contends that 80 percent of a school's success depends on two factors: the cognitive ability of the child and *the disposition he brings to class—not on texts, teachers or classroom size. If the brains and the will to learn are absent, no amount of spending on schools, teacher salaries, educational consultants or new texts will matter. A nation weary of wasting billions on unctuous educators who never deliver what they promise may be ready to hear some hard truths.*

This article explains some very important truths. Education starts at home. Study after study shows that children raised in homes with a mother and a father outperformed those children who were not. And study after study show that race has more to do with learning than does dollars spent on education. But the education unions continue to use the racial divide to ask for more and more money.

For a summary, let me use this email from a friend, Gaven K:

…my eyes do see the abuse, the disrespect, the control, the enslavement by government entities, U.S. included. Eckhart Tolle, the spiritual teacher who influenced me on to the path 10 years ago said some 90% of the suffering inflicted upon humans is not done by criminals locked up in jails, but by highly respected individuals [sitting in highly respected offices]… and I see that it is true—40% of my income goes straight into taxes….

Schools… ah, I don't even want to get started. Worse than prison cells in de-humanizing and mentally enslaving children at an early age, so they never speak up for themselves later. Destroyers of creativity, compassion, and care. Human beings in these systems are precious, worthwhile, divine even, but these systems are evil, evil, evil...

... please know I'm very much with you against further and further enslavement of the common American.

Chapter 3
Save America Now!

This chapter is an excerpt from my book, *Save America Now!* This is a summary of what "needs" to be done to save America.

If you are an American who has worked hard and saved and believed in the system, you are about to lose everything. So now is the perfect time to join the revolution to save America.

As said by Bob Dylan. "When you got nothing, then you got nothing to lose."

Hard-working Americans are about to lose everything.

The liberal tyrants are about to take all of it. They stole our individual savings in Social Security for their political programs. They stole our personal savings with inflation by printing an excessive amount of money. They stole freedom of religion. They stole the right to bear arms by taxing weapons and ammunition excessively. They stole the culture with the use of "political correctness." They stole our children with constant brainwashing on television, in the movies, and in their classrooms. They are taxing away the estates that we plan to leave to our children. They are handing our country to illegal immigrants. They killed the Constitution with rulings by activist judges. They killed independence in favor of a new world order. And now they are using the tyranny of the majority to implement full-fledged socialism with more government and more taxes.

Hard-working Americans are about to have nothing. "When you got nothing, then you got nothing to lose."

So now is the time to say:

Governments are instituted among men, deriving their just powers from the consent of the governed; that whenever any form of government becomes destructive of these ends, it is the right of the people to alter or to abolish it, and to institute new government.

It is time to join the revolution to *Save America Now!*

There is a temptation to select socialism and more government control for substantial portions of our private corporations as the solution to our problems. There is a temptation to succumb to the lure of a New World Order for the promise of world peace and the cause of saving the environment. But once our Constitution is compromised, there is no going back to the freedom that Americans have known for the last 250 years. The American dream will be gone.

There is a temptation to tax the rich and give it to the rest of the population. That redistribution of wealth is a losing proposition. It might help for a short amount of time. But the redistribution of wealth does not create any additional funds for the economy. It only moves the funds around. And redistribution of wealth is morally wrong because it is theft by the majority.

There is a temptation to remove religion from our values and replace religious values with secularism. That is one of the steps that leads to totalitarianism and tyranny.

But there is another way. There is hope. We can stop the cycle. We can save America now. The root causes of our current economic problems are from 50 years of liberal policies, and we can stop those policies if we have the will of our Founding Fathers.

It will take a revolution to save America because our politicians are too entrenched in the current political process to save America. Our political leaders are too wed to their positions to risk them to actually save our Constitution. Our politicians owe too much to special interest groups to actually do what is good for America first.

Those liberal politicians (most of them are lawyers) want this battle to be waged on their battlefield of talk, talk, talk in courtrooms and government chambers to distract the rest of us. So Americans need to move this fight from the battlefield of lawyers and politicians to the streets of America.

Tell it like it is to every American that you can: "Liberals are destroying America and we the people need to save America now." Do not allow any compromises to our Constitution or our values that chip away at freedom and liberty. Get rid of those moderate conservatives who think that compromising is a good thing.

Ravi Batra, the economics Ph.D from India, stated a theory that populations vote to replace democracy led by business people with socialism led by elite intellectuals. That socialism evolves into a chaotic environment, which is then replaced with a dictatorship to bring order to the chaos. That dictatorship is eventually replaced by businessmen who install democracy and capitalism again. And so the cycle continues. He goes on to state that the United States has remained in the democracy stage longer than any previous civilizations—more than 200 years.

The United States has been able to fend off the urge to move to the socialist stage each time it has been presented by intellectuals. But does the United States have the will to fend off socialism now? Will our current financial problems be exploited to justify more socialism and more industry nationalization? Will the environment and the fight against terrorism be used to justify a new world order—a world government that eliminates our protections from government in our Constitution?

Each of us needs to take a few minutes and read the Declaration of Independence and the Constitution. Read them slowly. Read them word for word. And then ask yourself what those words mean to you as an individual. Don't let other people influence you. Read them for yourself and decide for yourself.

Our Declaration and our Constitution state a premise that the individual is more important than the group. Independence— not interdependence, not co-dependence, but independence. The group is more important than the state. The state is more important than the federal government. Our country and its Constitution are more important than any implementation of a world government/order. And the Creator is more important than any of us. These concepts are very clear in our Declaration of "Independence" and in our Constitution. To defend and protect our Constitution is part of the oath of every government official, especially the Supreme Court, Congress, and the president.

We the people need to save those concepts. We need to save America now because our government leaders are not honoring their oaths of office.

Anyone who opposes these concepts must be treated as evil, as someone who is deliberately subverting America and its basic values as a traitor with all of the punishments that are due to a traitor.

The root causes of the ills in our economy today have evolved from 50 years of policies from the liberal portions of the Baby Boom generation. Let's review them:

An aging population. The average age in America has increased dramatically. Part of the reason is that the average American is living longer, but the major reason is that the birth rate decreased per the number of adults in America during the 70s and early 80s. That affects everything from increasing medical care costs to decreasing demand for products and decreasing the amount of available workers to pay for the social security of retired workers. This is a direct result of using zero population growth by liberals to justify abortion and to justify not having more children.

A lack of oil drilling or nuclear expansion. The United States currently imports $700 billion more in goods than it exports each year. That entire trade deficit is due to oil. That is five times greater than what was the expense for the Iraq war each year. It deflated the value of the dollar. It caused a 5 percent leakage to our money supply each year. It forced the United States to become a credit economy. This is a direct result of liberal actions to stop oil drilling, coal mining, and nuclear expansion for the last 30 years.

The "change" from a manufacturing economy to a service and government economy. The deep supply chains associated with manufacturing have been replaced with the single layer supply chains of service businesses and government. The reduction to the multiplier effect from this change over the last 40 years has been devastating. The loss in manufacturing jobs is the single largest reason for the decrease in the average wage per worker. The United States has changed from a GDP comprised 70 percent manufacturing to a GDP of 70 percent services and government. Local, state and federal taxes increased to a collective amount of 54 percent from every dollar earned by the average worker in America to pay for the expansion to governments. To compensate for the loss to the money supply from less manufacturing and increased taxes, new financial instruments were created like sub-prime mortgages, and easy qualification credit cards. While these added more money to the overall money supply, those instruments also delayed the onset of our economic decline, which was caused by the change from a manufacturing economy to a services/government economy. A growing, vibrant economy is driven by innovation, manufacturing and marketing and not by accountants, governments or lawyers. If the United States is being led by accountants and lawyers, the United States is in trouble. Next comes socialism, then chaos, followed by totalitarian government to correct the chaos, and finally death to the American dream as we know it as a direct result of actions by labor unions, government, and the liberal assault against business.

The **demise of traditional values,** especially within the family unit. Men abdicated their responsibilities as fathers. The increase in children raised by single parents has been accompanied by increased crime, lower scholastic achievement and fewer engineers. The cost to our society and economy has been huge. The demise of traditional values has also produced other negative results including the unethical habits of our business and government leaders. As religion and traditional values have been eliminated from our society and schools, so the ethics of our leaders have fallen. As liberals justified abortion, preached that a single parent could raise children as well as a family with a mother and a father, pushed socialism with concepts like, "It Takes a Village," and pushed for a secular society; the negative impact to our society has been devastating.

We Americans are at a turning point today. Can the United States remain the beacon of democracy and capitalism or will it fade into history like all the other societies? If it becomes more socialistic, it will eventually end in chaos and totalitarianism. If you think this cannot happen in your lifetime, well, then you only need to look at how Russia went through the entire four stages of the cycle in the last 20 years. Russia went from a communist dictatorship in 1988, to a democratic government with capitalistic principles in 1991, to the election of socialist politicians in the late '90s until the chaos—caused by the elected labor leaders in Russia in the early 2000's and was replaced by the election of Putin, a KGB dictator.

Today more than ever, as Washington, Jefferson, Teddy Roosevelt, and so many of our great leaders have said in the past, the character of the leader is more important than any single political issue. Issues change but character remains, so the critical element for Americans should be an evaluation of the character of our leaders. Teddy Roosevelt was quite clear when he said: "Always look at character first."

We Americans need to elect leaders who have the right character and experience to make the right decisions for the short term and the long term for our society.

We need a surge strategy to help save America in the short run.

1. We as a nation need to drill new oil fields and build new refineries, mine for more coal, and build new

nuclear facilities now. This will create jobs with no money needed from the government and it will help secure independence for America now … not at some undetermined time in the future.

2. Taxes on our manufacturing corporations need to be cut in half to keep them at home.

3. We need to implement a new economic incentive package. Our federal government should spend $100 billion on placing orders for additional manufactured goods that are made in the United States by U.S. corporations with American-made components. We need a one hundred billion dollar "New Deal" for the twenty-first century. This $100 billion will create 1 million new manufacturing jobs and might add 1.5 trillion dollars to the economy because of the multiplier effect from manufactured goods. One hundred billion is only 3 percent of our federal budget. Compare this $100 billion to the $1.75 trillion that has been spent by the current administration to help the economy. The $1.75 trillion has been wasted on service and government with no economic return. That money is lost. The money should be spent by government as a consumer of manufactured products. It should not be spent to add more service and government employees. And the government should not ever be involved in ownership of American corporations.

4. As the war in Iraq winds down, we need to be careful to not use that money for service programs. The expenditures for Iraq actually helped our manufacturing industries. The military buys clothing, vehicles, guns, and other things that are manufactured in the United

States. If that money is used for government social programs, then we exacerbate our economic problems by moving more money from the manufacturing industry to service programs. That money needs to be spent on goods manufactured in America and not diverted to social service programs or financial bailouts.

5. America needs to put an end to the bailout mentality that the government will always rescue those who commit poor judgment and will bail them out of bankruptcy, debt and the consequences of their decisions. We need to use our freedom responsibly to carefully manage our risk as responsible free individuals. No business should be given any money from the government to help it survive. They will stop their constant lobby efforts and contributions to politicians.

In the long term, we need a revolution to change the course set by the Baby Boom liberals during the last 40 years in order to save America and all that America represents.

1. We need to *create a culture of life* to lower the average age of Americans. We need to encourage more births by changing our values and putting the right incentives in place. We need to discourage abortion. We need to encourage marriage and to facilitate the ability of one parent to stay at home to raise the children if that is what a family desires. We need to discourage divorce so all children are raised by a mother and a father. We can do that by changing our tax system. We could also lower the average age of Americans by encouraging the migration

of skilled immigrants who bring their families to live and work in America so they do not need to send money home.

2. We need to foster a return to *a moral America*, a religious America. We need to take the immoral, unethical greed out of America that causes so many people to put selfish needs ahead of the needs of all America. We need to remove envy as a tool politicians use to separate Americans into classes that covet the lifestyles and wealth of others. We need to allow more school vouchers so parents can choose to send their children to schools with curricula that include more about the impact of religions on history and more about morals and ethics. We need to make education a parent's "right to choose," just like liberals made abortion a woman's right to choose.

3. We need to *bring manufacturing back* to America so that it grows to 50 percent of GDP. This will increase jobs and the average wage per worker. The longer supply chain of manufacturing will multiply jobs throughout our economy. We need to lower corporate taxes. We need to say "no" to the demands of union executives and government bureaucrats who chase manufacturing out of the United States. Unions have an honorable historical place in America, but it is the job of our government, especially the president, to stop actions or policies that will harm the U.S. economy, like a law that would allow unions to hold votes without a secret ballot. We need to educate more students in engineering, science and math. Let's take some of the scholarships

for liberal arts and convert them to scholarships for the hard sciences. And we need to reduce capital gains taxes and dividend taxes to encourage more investment in American manufacturing companies. The federal, state and local governments of the United States need to cut back and spend less on social services so they can spend more on manufactured goods and construction projects. The government needs to learn to "just say no" to service spending.

4. We need to **save Social Security**. Social Security was meant to be a government administered annuity program for the individual contributor with the addition of employer contributions. We need to restore that simple objective for our young people and also make good on the obligations owed to our older folks.

5. We need to **achieve independence, not just energy independence, but total independence.** Those who want a new world government want all of us in the world to be interdependent. They really do not want the United States to be independent. They want us to need the oil of the Middle East and the labor and manufactured goods of Asia. They want us to look to Europe for banking and finance. They want an interdependent world with one government. It is up to each of us in the United States to resist them. It is up to each of us to force our government to make the United States be independent of the world, yet participate in world events. We need to start with energy. The United States needs to be energy independent now by drilling more oil fields, mining more coal, and building more nuclear facilities. Then use the profits and taxes

received from additional oil, coal, and nuclear power production to help fund research and development of alternate sources of energy so that all the energy needs of the United States are supplied internally and can become manufacturing independent. The United States needs to have the capability to manufacture all of its needed manufactured goods. Those politicians who talk about United States' independence and yet oppose oil drilling, coal mining, nuclear expansion, oppose lower taxes on manufacturing companies, oppose stopping the destruction to American business by unions, and continue to divert more money to service organizations and/or government are just plain lying to America about wanting the United States to be independent. They are traitors and should be treated as such. Strength in the world arena comes from independence ... not interdependence. We have a Declaration of Independence ... not one of interdependence.

6. We need to **reform the tax structure** in America. We need a tax structure that collects funds to pay for the government expenses documented in the Constitution and to motivate the behavior of the population. We need a flat tax rate for all Americans and then a universal deduction system that causes lower taxes for those who earn less based on their deductions. We need an amendment to our Constitution that will end the use of taxes by our politicians for class warfare, for redistributing wealth, and for perpetuating their own power by funding partisan political groups with government funds.

7. We need to *implement a mandatory service program for all young Americans.* We need to bring the spirit of our WWII generation back to the United States without having a war to do it.

8. We need *judges who will honor the law* and not let their personal values cloud their judicial decisions. Our Constitution and our laws are living documents because they have processes for changing themselves as the people dictate those changes, not because a judge determines that a change is needed. A judge who makes a change without a mandate from the people negates the democratic process of amendment as set forth in the U.S. Constitution and our state constitutions.

9. We need to *listen to our Founding Fathers.* Honor thy mother and father. We need to honor our Founding Fathers. They deliberately said, "All men are created equal." They did not say all men are equal. They did not say all men should be equal. They only said that "All men are created equal"—nothing more. They said that our rights to life, liberty and pursuit of happiness come from God, not man, government or some other group.

10. And last, we need to *elect candidates with good moral fiber*—good character. Those who divert the review of a candidate's character to other topics, or who impede the ability of We the People to obtain all the facts concerning character, or who slant the facts about character are enemies of America. Character must be the first consideration about any leader, not issues. Trust. If you cannot trust a candidate, then no statements about issues can be trusted. Look at Obama as the example. He lied

during the campaign and now he is not honoring many of his campaign promises. Character counts. Those who deflected inspection of his character are traitors to America. We need to trust our leaders like we trusted the WWII generation. The decisions that our leaders make today will affect the world that we leave for our children and grandchildren. Will it be freedom and the American dream or will it be socialism leading to chaos and a totalitarian government?

Since writing *Save America Now,* liberals have done more to destroy America than ever could have been imagined. At the same time, conservatives are winning some battles, especially the Tea Parties, so my original list of solutions to save America needs some revision.

1. Politicians and economists are discussing how benefits need to be cut back for retirees in order to keep Social Security solvent. That is not true. Look at the wages for government employees and the number of them. Since government employees make 30% more than their counterparts in the private sector, their compensations can be cut to more than offset the deficits in the Social Security trust. The Federal Government stole the money from our pensions in the Social Security Trust and used it for political projects, so the federal government needs to figure out how to pay it back. One way is to cut government employee compensation. A three percent cut to all government workers would provide the $30 billion per year to keep Social Security solvent with no reductions to benefits to retirees.

2. Much discussion is devoted on how to implement a fair tax system—a tax system that eliminates the punitive progressive tax rates. Well, today more than half of Americans pay no federal income taxes and more than a third of Americans receive payments from the government. That is not fair by any means. It is political bribery. The USA can implement a fair system by either abandoning the income method of taxation or by taxing everyone at the same rate and allowing for enough deductions for dependents so that low income families will still pay no taxes.

3. Republicans and Democrats are discussing repeal of some of the items in the health "insurance" law. This is exactly what Alinsky coached liberals to do. Push. Push. Push. Then fall back. Pushing and then compromising will eventually give liberals everything that they want. Some of the total is better than none. Then they will use that partial position to gain more until eventually all of the liberal healthcare agenda is accomplished. If Alinsky was right, then the only way to stop any of the health "insurance" law is to repeal all of it. No compromises. Those Republicans and Democrats who talk about partial repeals are capitulating to the liberal strategy.

4. Manufacturing and energy are the keys to ending the trade deficits that are draining the money supply from America. This government is not serious about fixing either one of these problems. It is obvious that a deal has been made with other nations that the USA will be the food provider for the world and then will purchase oil and manufactured products from abroad. Otherwise,

the USA would be attacking the impediments to energy and manufacturing. This deal stretches back at least forty years through Republican and Democrat administrations. The impediments to manufacturing competitiveness include not enough engineering college graduates, too high of labor costs, and incremental taxes that roll up throughout the manufacturing supply chain. The impediments to energy include the need for more nuclear sites, more oil drilling, and more coal mining. As long as liberals are in control (Democrats and Republicans) who are more loyal to the world order than to the USA, then nothing will be done to correct manufacturing or energy. As financial problems emerge, their solutions will continue to be just throwing more money at them. So my recommendation is to stop any and all bail outs to unions, to businesses who are in trouble, and to the financial industry. Then watch all of them get on board with how to correct the energy and manufacturing problems so they can also stay viable as secondary beneficiaries.

5. Governor Christie of New Jersey has shown America how to deal with the NEA (teachers union). He makes every one of their demands visible. He uses the internet, TV, town hall meetings, and open discussions to expose how teachers are selfish to the point of destruction. If every town, city, county, and state would do the same with their teachers, then teachers would stop their selfish demands that are destroying our educational system.

6. Term limits will end the "professional politicians." Does anyone remember all of those Republicans who were elected in 1994 as part of the "Contract with America?" Does anyone remember that contract included a pledge from all of those representatives that they would not serve any longer than three terms of two years for each? And how many did it? A total of four. A total of 4 kept that pledge of no more than 3 terms. A sign was held up at the September 11, 2010 Tea Party in Washington, DC that read "10 or 2 and then out." It is simple. For any one elected position, ten years or two terms, whichever is more, and then no more. We need to pass an amendment to the Constitution that states ten years or two terms, whichever is more and then no more for all federal elected positions. And until an amendment is passed, then "vote em out at 10 or 2, whichever is more." Vote any of them out who are running for more than ten years or two terms, whichever is more. And it doesn't matter what party. It doesn't matter how good of a guy each one is. "Vote em all out at 10 years or 2 terms, whichever is more!" This will help eliminate the ruling class in America.

7. Make judges accountable to "we the people." If a society can place limits on polygamy and sodomy, then it can also place them on gay marriage and other social issues. The judges who overstep their authority as stated in state and federal constitutions should be impeached. Often. Impeach lots of them. Often. As Reagan pointed out, governments need to fear the people, not the other way around. And that includes judges. "We the

people" need to impeach them until the legislatures do it as our representatives. Conservatives should contribute funding to legal groups who are as strong at impeachment of liberal judges as the ACLU is at promoting the agenda of liberals. And also: after watching the appointments of Sotomayor and Kagan, it is obvious that we need an amendment so that all Supreme Court nominations are ratified by "We the People," and not the Senate. Presidents will then think twice before nominating people like Sotomayor and Kagan.

8. Drill for more oil, build nuclear sites, and dig for more coal now! Energy companies will gladly do this with their own funds. It will not cost anything to American tax payers. It will create more jobs without government funds. And it will help create more security for Americans. With the fall of Egypt, Yemen, and most of the Mideast to Muslim radical organizations, nothing can be more important than for the USA to become "independent." Yet, the USA government continues to ignore this major issue to American security and the economy. The lack of driving the USA towards "independence" in this situation of unstated war with radical Muslims should be considered to be treason against the USA.

This is from an article in the *American Thinker* of February 5, 2011, titled "Obama Well Knows What Chaos He Has Unleashed" By Victor Sharpe :

Not content with creating havoc in the U.S. economy, setting Americans against each other, and forcing through a health reform act which has nothing to do with health but everything to do with the redistribution of wealth and an immense increase in governmental interference, our President has now opened a Pandora's Box in the Middle East. It may well usher in a catastrophe not seen since World War II.

From his notorious Cairo speech to the present, President Obama speaks, and disaster follows. Some commentators believe that President Obama and Secretary of State Clinton are so utterly naïve as to make themselves unable to understand what will happen in Egypt as a result of their undermining of the Mubarak regime.

The question is justifiably asked: Do they truly believe that the next regime that comes to power will have the interests of the U.S. and the West at heart?

My fear is that Obama is not naïve at all, but he instead knows only too well what he is doing, for he is eagerly promoting Islamic power in the world while diminishing the West and Israel however much innocent blood flows as a result.

Inevitably, sooner or later, the Muslim Brotherhood will take power, usher in a barbaric Islamist power in Egypt that will control the Suez Canal, and show no mercy to its own people or its perceived foes.

So now we see what the present incumbent in the White House has wrought, and so can our few remaining allies. They must now wonder what confidence they can ever have in any future alliance with the United States.

We should be aware of what endemic Islamic violence has wrought in the past. For example, assassinations of Arab leaders are not an infrequent occurrence. After the 1948 Arab-

*Israel War, the King of Jordan, Abdullah, was murdered by
followers of the Muslim fanatic, the Mufti of Jerusalem.*

*The Egyptian Prime Minister, Nokrashi Pasha, was also
struck down. The forces behind the killings were elements of
both Arab socialist movements and the Muslim Brotherhood.
Today, in the streets of Cairo, we have an unholy alliance of
the current radical left with the same Muslim Brotherhood.*

*The Suez Canal is a major lifeline for the economies
of Europe and the United States. It has been the source of
political disruption in the past, as it may well be in the near
future. And the Muslim Brotherhood may soon control it. As
always, the past is our guidepost to the future.*

Our leaders know what they need to do to save America, so how
do we the people make them do it?

Chapter 4
Five Rules

Okay, so how can each "individual" help stop the destruction of America?

Edmund Burke said it so plainly: "The only thing necessary for the triumph of evil is for good men (and women) to do nothing (paraphrased)."

To stop evil, good people need to take action against it. To compromise with what you know to be wrong, to tolerate what you know to be wrong, or to ignore what you know to be wrong is to allow evil to thrive. To stop evil, good men (and women) need to do something. They need to take action against evil.

All too often, conservatives think in nouns. They use terms like unemployment, assets, family, country, money, liberty, and freedom; but conservatives forget that nothing happens until some action is taken. Conservatives need to think in verbs. They need to think in action words. Then conservatives will take action.

Save
As discussed in *Save America Now*, to conserve is to save. Conservatives save.

How many conservatives see their mission as saving America? How many Americans are willing to risk their lives, their fortunes, and their families to save America as our Founding Fathers pledged in the Declaration of Independence?

Those judges who refused to hear the Obama natural born citizenship case were certainly not willing to risk their lives, their fortunes, or their families. They were not willing to risk their positions in society to resolve this ongoing doubt about the natural born citizenship of Obama. While they dismiss this as being insignificant, it goes to the premise of contract law and the terms of the contract between the government and we the people called the Constitution of the United States.

This "certificate of live birth" provided by Barack Hussein at the end of April 2011 proves that he inherited Kenya citizenship from his father and his own books admit that he inherited Indonesian citizenship from his step father. So did Barack Hussein Obama use foreign citizenship as an adult? What is on his college documents and on his passports? Why did he spend millions of dollars to seal all of those documents?

This whole birth certificate thing distracted America from the real issue. It did exactly what Obama and the liberal media cartel wanted. It seems to me like Donald Trump either played into it or led us there deliberately.

Barack Hussein cannot be president if he *ever* held dual/foreign citizenship as an adult. 8 USC 1481 is clear. Obama knows this. Congress knows this. The courts know this. They are all distracting us by focusing on his birth site and his birth certificate. So what is in those sealed documents from his colleges and passports?

Many politicians believe that if it is true that Obama is disqualified from being able to be president because of dual citizenship that riots and chaos will be the result. Their short-sighted reasoning is helping to destroy our Constitution. History will disclose the truth and that might just be the last straw that ends any trust in our government, and the motivations of people like Donald Trump.

Maybe judges are not taking this case because they are willing to risk their own lives and fortunes, but not their families. Just like for Woody in Chapter 1, the threat of harm to a family member might be just too much to ask from our judges.

How important is America to each of us? Does each of us have a mindset that saving our country today is as important as it was for those who fought in WWII? The protection of America is an ongoing task. Saving America from its external enemies and internal enemies is an ongoing, perpetual task. It will continue forever. Just as religious leaders wake up each day with the mission of saving souls, the conservative needs to wake up each day with the mission to do something, however so small, to save what our Founding Fathers gave us. They gave us a Declaration of Independence—not one of "dependence"—and a Constitution to limit the authority of the federal government.

In his book, *The Conscience of a Conservative*, Barry Goldwater made this observation:

And that is what the Constitution is: a system of restraints against the natural tendency of government to expand in the direction of absolutism. We all know the main components of the system. The first is the limitation of the federal government's authority to specific, delegated powers. The second, a corollary of the first, is the reservation to the States and the people of all power not delegated to the federal government. The third is a careful division of the federal government's power among three separate branches. The forth is the prohibition against impetuous alteration of the system – namely, Article V's tortuous, but wise, amendment procedures.

While the radical is here to use change to seize power for the radical, the conservative needs to look at the radical and say that conservatives are here to save America from those actions of the radical that will harm America. Conservatives are here to save our Constitution.

Challenge

For so long, liberals have gone unchallenged. Conservatives were afraid of being called racists, of offending others, of seeming like they were not compassionate, and of being accused of causing conflict. For so long, conservative parents allowed their liberally brainwashed children to dominate conversations while those same children lived off funds provided by the conservative parents.

The results are obvious. Government has grown. Taxes have grown. And the power of liberal leaders has grown.

On February 19, 2009, Rick Santelli challenged the government and Obama on *CNBC* in a rousing talk from the floor of the stock market. His comments circulated all over the Internet. It is still available on YouTube. Millions of Americans watched him challenge the government. Millions of Americans watched him call for Tea Parties all across America. Millions watched him point out what so many people wanted to say out loud, but remained silent. He said that the government did not know what it was doing. It was spending too much money. He then turned to everyone around him and asked: "How many of you people want to pay your neighbors' mortgages?"

Rick Santelli was the first to say that the emperor has no clothes.

In August of that same year, Tea Party people from all across the country filled town halls to challenge the actions of their congressmen and senators. From the comments of Rick Santelli, the Tea Parties were born. In those town hall meetings, people asked their representatives tough questions about taxes, spending, and new government entitlements. Then 2 million of them filed into Washington, DC in September 2009 to add their protest against government growth and spending and taxes. It was the largest single demonstration in Washington in history. They repeated it in September 2010.

The Tea Party people carried their message all across the county: No more taxes, no additional government. The Decocratic Party did not listen. They passed the healthcare "insurance" legislation even though all polls showed that almost two-thirds of Americans did not want it. Democrats continued to pass legislation that cost more and more for Americans. The result is that the Democratic Party incurred the largest amount of losses in the Federal and in the State elections of 2010 since the losses of the Republican Party in 1932. Democratic lawyers who dominated the national legislature were replaced by working people. 33 of the newly elected Republican Congressmen were small business owners. So far, 25 state Democrats have switched to the Republican Party.

Shortly after the November, 2010 election, Mitch McConnell, head of the Republicans in the Senate, stated that he would not support a ban on earmarks in Congressional legislation. Millions of Americans took to the Internet to challenge him. They posted on every website imaginable. World Net Daily, TownHall, Red State, Atlah, NewsMax all carried articles about how he did not get the message in the November election that America wants to end government spending. For several days, *Drudge* carried McConnell stories in the front page. Millions of postings by average Americans on *Free Republic* were merciless. Americans were angry. And McConnell heard them. Within two weeks, McConnell changed his stance and said that he would block any legislation that included earmarks. *The Washington Post* covered the story on his "sudden reversal" on November 16, 2010.

This is the second rule for conservatives: *Challenge*.

Challenge everything and anything that does not seem right. Because the conservatives did not challenge the disparagement of George W. Bush, the liberals got away with demonizing him and carried that demonization into the 2008 elections. Because conservatives in Congress did not challenge the nomination of Sotomayor for the Supreme Court, the liberals were able to put a person on the Supreme Court who clearly had anti-American writings and actions in her past.

Because conservatives did not challenge those courts that banned prayer in schools, the impact of religion on America is being wiped from the history textbooks and from classroom discussions.

Because conservatives did not challenge the status of the natural born citizenship of Barack Hussein Obama during the election cycle, no court is brave enough to hear the case now that Obama is in office.

Because conservatives and John McCain did not adequately challenge Obama's history and his associations with Wright, Ayres, Rezko, Soros, and so many others during the election process, most of America did not understand the true philosophies of Obama until after he was elected.

Because conservatives did not adequately challenge the spending of Democrats since they took control of Congress in the November 2006 elections, the deficit of the national government increased from $160 billion to $1.7 trillion and unemployment increased from 4.6 percent to close to 10 percent after the liberals, especially Obama, promised that their spending would keep unemployment under 8 percent.

When the radicals are allowed to practice the rules presented by Saul Alinsky without challenge, America loses.

The second rule for conservatives is to challenge. Challenge everything. Challenge anything. If it seems strange, out of line or incorrect, challenge it. When conservatives let the liberals intimidate them—keep them from challenging liberal actions—then all of America loses.

Talk the Talk

It's okay to say "no." If a drug pusher handed free drugs to your children, would you tell your children to say no? Of course. So when the liberals accuse conservatives of being the "no" people, then conservatives should embrace it as a compliment because liberals are addicting Americans to dependence on government. Liberals are pushers. Addiction is bad. Just say "no."

Just like saying "no," conservatives need to speak up. Conservatives need to speak up loudly.

How often have you listened to a discussion where you have totally disagreed with what was said, but you kept silent? This happens so often when liberals are part of the discussion. Liberals talk over any disagreement so that the disagreement cannot be heard—just as they were instructed to do by Saul Alinsky. And in the process, the surrounding listeners begin to think that the liberal opinion is the general consensus.

Have you ever listened to Debbie Wasserman Schultz, Jewish Democrat Congresswoman from Florida, in a debate with a Republican on TV? The Republican barely gets a chance to speak. Even when it is not her turn to talk, Debbie talks over the Republican. And if the Republican tries to talk, then Debbie talks even louder. Debbie is just practicing what Alinsky instructed her to do.

Just look how liberals sold the world on global cooling in the 80s, then global warming in the 90s, and now global climate change. They talked over any opposition until they could claim that the global scheme *du jour* was the general consensus of the scientific community. And for each situation of "cooling" or "warming" or "climate change" their solution has been the same—reduce the population and reduce the use of oil. So maybe their real thrust is to reduce population and reduce the use of oil, and maybe they are just looking for scientific justification— any justification—cooling, warming, or just change, so they can blame it on population and oil. Any person looking at this history of cooling, then warming, then climate change can tell that the liberal logic is inconsistent and that liberals are just seeking justification for what liberals ultimately want to do— reduce the world population and ban the use of oil.

But who could hear the objections to the liberal logic when the liberals were so loud? Who could hear the arguments about inconsistency when liberals shouted those arguments into silence? And who could hear any opposition when liberals dominated every conversation in the media and in the classrooms?

The media had America believing that America wanted the changes being legislated by the Democratic Congress of 2007 to 2011. They had America believing that America wanted Obamacare and all the other Obama programs. Every discussion was on how to implement the Democratic agenda—not about if it should be implemented.

Despite the polls by Zogby, Pew, Rasmussen, and Gallup that pointed out that two-thirds of America did not want the Obamacare legislation, that America is mostly a conservative country, and that America is concerned about the growth in government; the Democratic controlled Congress of 2007 to 2011 continued the liberal agenda with the full blessings of the media. If anyone listened to Keith Olbermann or Chris Matthews or Brian Williams or Katie Couric or Jon Stewart, then that person would probably believe that the liberal views were the consensus in America.

Then something happened in America in 2009—the Tea Parties. Tea Party people spoke up in town halls. They spoke up in small cities. They spoke up all across America until two million of them shouted, "Can you hear us now?" They shouted it at the government in Washington, DC in September 2009, and then again in September 2010. The Tea Parties were loud. They were vocal. They could not be ignored. Many incumbent Republicans lost their seats in the primaries because they would not listen. Then the largest number of Democrats in almost 100 years lost their combined seats in the Senate, House of Representatives, and local governments because they listened to themselves instead of what was happening in the streets in America.

When conservatives talk the talk—loudly—then they make a difference. When they allow the liberals to dominate the conversations, then all of America loses.

Walk the Walk

Conservatives see people as individuals. Liberal followers of Saul Alinsky see people as masses to be organized and to be used to give themselves power—blacks, single women, government workers, college students, and Hispanics. Liberals organize them and make promises to them, to gain power for themselves.

So the first thing that conservatives need to do is to build relationships one at a time.

Often, conservatives are called the silent majority, but that is only because liberals cannot hear conservatives as conservatives discuss things one-on-one.

Frank Wolf has been the Congressional Representative for my district for more than twenty years of living in Northern Virginia. He is one of the last remaining conservatives who were elected to the House of Representatives as part of the Reagan revolution.

Frank walked the walk. He gave me private, one-on-one audiences on three occasions. In 2001, he stepped into a situation to help our small family owned company. He never asked me what group was represented by me. Frank never asked me my political affiliation, and he never received any money from me for any of his campaigns—ever. He treated me with respect as an individual just because he represented me. He did not see me as part of some group or as a lobbyist who would provide him some political donations. Frank walked the walk.

Compare that to those who call themselves conservatives, yet pander to groups. They are not conservatives.

Saul Alinsky was the one who instructed liberals to seize power by organizing mass groups. Conservatives believe that the individual is most important. Now that may seem like a losing proposition for conservatives. And it is a losing proposition unless lots of individuals refuse to be organized. Those people who will not be organized are conservatives. And conservatives make up the majority of America. We are individuals.

Conservatives need to walk the walk. Conservatives need to display their conservative colors just the same as displaying their college colors, or their home team football colors, or their children's school colors.

And what are those colors? How about the American flag to start? Or how about religious symbols? Or how about bumper stickers that call for reduced government? In 2008, the liberals flooded the world with Obama paraphernalia 24/7—all Obama—and the world thought that all of America wanted Obama.

Walk the walk. Bob Bennett (Utah), Cochran (Miss.), Collins (Maine), Inhofe (Okla.), Lugar (Ind.), Murkowski (Alaska), Shelby (Ala.) and Voinovich (Ohio) had an opportunity to vote for a moratorium on earmarks in the Senate. Granted, earmarks are less than 1 percent of federal spending, but earmarks symbolize all that is wrong with how government takes care of special interest "groups." These supposed conservatives all voted against the moratorium. They refused to show their conservative colors. They did not walk the walk.

It is not good enough to talk a good game. Conservatives need to walk the walk.

This letter was sent by me.

Open Letter to:
Congressman John Boehner
Congressman Eric Cantor
Congressman Frank Wolf
US House of Representatives

Washington, DC
January 24, 2011

Dear Sirs,

We the people elected you Republicans to be the controlling party of the US House of Representatives last Nov, 2010 to hold the Democrats and Barack Hussein Obama accountable. The Democrat controlled House of 2008 did not vet Mr. Obama. After promising to be "transparent," Obama was allowed by the Democrat House of 2008 to not be "transparent" about being a "natural born" citizen. The 2008 House did not vet him.

Your most current comments about this are very disturbing. Are you going to vet him? The president of the United States must be a natural born citizen to qualify to be president. The ways to lose natural born citizenship status are detailed in 8 USC 1481. One way is becoming naturalized in another country.

Are you going to inspect his long form birth certificate, his college applications, and his previous passports? Do any of those documents show him to have a dual or foreign citizenship that would have caused him to have lost his natural born status? Almost 2/3 of America think that there is something wrong with his citizenship. So are you going to vet him to put this issue to rest?

You took an oath of office to protect and defend the Constitution of the United States. So are you going to do that concerning the "natural born" status of Barack Hussein Obama (Barry Soetoro)?

Please read the last line of the Declaration of Independence. It states:

With a firm reliance on the protection of divine Providence, we mutually pledge to each other our Lives, our fortunes and our sacred Honor.

Are you willing to risk your lives, your fortunes, and your sacred honor to protect and defend the Constitution of the United States? Are you willing to risk your families?

This letter is being copied to America so that everyone will be watching you to see if you walk the walk or just talk the talk?

Michael Master

If every conservative talked to ten independents and/or moderate liberals continually in the next year about important issues that affect America, then no amount of media bias could overwhelm the conversations of those conservatives. One-on-one—as individuals. And the media would not be able to undo with its mass techniques what conservatives would accomplish one-on-one.

Every spring, a group of us small business owners and executives go on a low budget golf trip to Myrtle Beach, South Carolina. On that trip, we discuss lots of things—kids, colleges for our kids, the government, baseball teams, everything. Last year, we had a discussion about how the low birth rates in the 70s and 80s were affecting the housing market of 2008, 2009, and 2010, and how that was affecting so many ancillary markets like the furniture market and the home appliance market. Several guys who voted for Democrats in the last election said that they had never heard that a root cause to the housing market problems was because of the low number of births of forty years ago. They remembered how liberals, especially feminists, pushed zero population growth and abortion, but they did not understand its effect on the economy of today until our conversations.

During the rest of 2010, we all watched and discussed continuously how the government struggled to cure the economy with bail outs and debt—and how it never addressed the issue of low demand from a decreased set of consumers between forty and fifty-five years old. We watched a government struggle to address economic issues with solutions that had nothing to do with the root causes to those problems. Those who voted for Obama in 2008 slowly realized that his administration either doesn't know what it is doing or it is deliberately using the economic crisis to justify its political agenda. They got their new information from our one-on-one discussions, not from the media or the government. As a result, half of them who voted for Democrats in 2008 voted for Republicans in the 2010 election.

Those arguments that persuaded those independents and moderate Democrats to look closely at the ineptness of the government were one-on-one ... as individuals. One-on-one discussions require that conservatives are informed and that they share that information.

The first step in walking the walk is treating others as individuals ... not as part of groups. That is the first step in being conservative. The next step in walking the walk is acting on conservative principles like voting as conservatives and living within economic boundaries. And the last step in walking the walk is persuading others one-on-one to look at things from the conservative perspective.

That is walking the walk.

Compromise Selfishly—

only when conservative principles gain from such compromise

Often conservatives give up positions on some things in order to gain positions on other things. When George W. Bush asked for funding for the Iraq invasion after 9/11, the Democratic controlled Senate attached stipulations for spending that they wanted. The Republicans agreed and Bush signed it. The result was that the deficit rose to $400 billion from the surplus that was left by a Republican Congress of 1995-2001. Those new programs that were implemented for Democrats cannot be cut without agreement from the Democrats in Congress unless Republicans gain control of Congress and the White House because a Democratic president will just veto the changes. That is a very difficult task. So spending increased and government salaries increased.

To the graduating class of the Harrow School in 1941, Winston Churchill said: "Never give in—never, never, never, never, in nothing great or small, large or petty, never give in except to convictions of honor and good sense."

When the nomination of Sotomayor was allowed to leave the Senate Judiciary Committee, Lindsay Graham compromised. He allowed the misgivings about Sotomayor to be subjugated to his desire to look fair even though the pounds of documentation showed her to be dramatically in opposition to all conservative positions, showed her to be an activist judge who would base judgment from outside of the four corners of the Constitution, and showed her to have anti-American sentiments. The Sotomayor appointment to the Supreme Court cannot be undone without impeachment. And the chance of that is slim. So that compromise by Graham cost conservatives gravely for potentially a long time.

The lesson learned from this is that conservatives cannot ever compromise in one area to get what they want in another area. It is too hard to reverse the compromise. And if a compromise should happen that moves the current state to B from A, then conservatives should only allow future compromises that move the current state back closer to A.

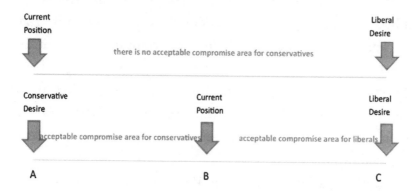

This rule takes much discipline. It requires that conservatives understand what the conservative position is. It also requires that the true conservative inspect every item in any deal to make sure that a compromise has not been imbedded to move the current state away from the conservative position.

On November 29, 2010, Barack Hussein Obama announced that he would implement a pay freeze on all federal government employees for two years. The union leaders staged a show of objection to make the general public feel that they were upset with it. As posted by the Bureau of Labor and Statistics, employees in the private sector have experienced a loss in wages in the time period of 2007 to 2011 when Democrats controlled Congress while the pay for government employees increased at a compounded rate of four percent per year. And as stated earlier in this book, government employees are paid substantially more money than their counterparts in the private sector— approximately 30 percent per job.

Obama was trying to present himself as a compromiser who was brokering a compromise between the union leaders and conservatives. The union leaders acted out their part of outrage to help Obama look like he was in the middle. But once again, Obama and the union leaders were deceiving America.

So what did a pay freeze mean for government employees? Nothing. It maintained the current situation for government workers and liberals who press for more government. It kept things at position B. On a net present value basis relative to the pay for employees in the private sector, the freeze actually increased the gap between the pay of government workers and private sector workers because the employees in the private sector had lost income.

The *Federal Times* of December 6, 2010 pointed out that Obama only froze the cost of living portion of pay raises. The adjustments for service years would continue so the amount saved from a cost of living freeze was actually quite small. But Obama made his announcement sound like all pay increases would be frozen.

Freezing the cost of living portion of pay was a joke. What cost of living increase was there in a recession—especially when pay in the private sector had decreased?

Conservatives should have denounced the pay freeze for government workers as a scam and asked for a pay reduction that would make government employees equal in pay to what is paid for the same jobs in the private sector. Conservatives should have asked for a 30% reduction to pay for government workers. That is position A. Then a compromise would have been some/any pay reductions to government employees rather than a pay freeze on only the cost of living portion of their pay. Instead, Eric Cantor and his cohorts applauded Obama. Cantor was more interested in appearing to be cooperative with the administration than upholding conservative principles. Cantor sold out.

For most of 2010, Obama and Clinton (Hillary) pressed the U.S. Senate to approve the Strategic Arms Reduction Treaty (START). It is a treaty between Russia and the USA to decrease the number of warheads of each. It also allows each country to inspect each other's missile facilities. John Kyl, Senator from Arizona, asked the Senate to delay any approval until all of the treaty could be debated. Instead, close to a dozen Republican senators agreed to "compromise" with Obama and voted to approve START. The Republican Senators from Tennessee voted for it because they got a couple billion dollars worth of spending targeted at Tennessee from Obama. They sold out the long-term interests of America for short term spending gains.

In review, the Russians now have total access to the locations of our missile system. What is even worse is that information will eventually be leaked to any and all enemies of the USA like Iran and China.

In the *Telegraph* of December 29, 2010, Peter Foster quotes the Minister for National Defense of China: "In the coming five years, our military will push forward preparations for military conflict in every strategic direction," said Liang Guanglie in an interview published by several state-backed newspapers in China. "We may be living in peaceful times, but we can never forget war, never send the horses south or put the bayonets and guns away."

China acts like a young, vibrant, country while the liberally led USA continues to deal, negotiate, and compromise like an old, dying, country. How does the START treaty make the USA any safer against the Chinese? It doesn't. As a matter of fact, the START treaty with Russia could make the U.S. more vulnerable to the Chinese and Iran and, and, and…

What did those Republican Senators get for compromising that was so important to them that they sold out the defense of the U.S.? Those Senators from Tennessee—Alexander and Corker—voted for START because Obama promised them several billions of dollars worth of government spending in Tennessee. That compromise—that "deal"—could be deadly to America. In Investors.com on December 8, 2010, the authors of *Make No More Faustian Pacts With The Left* made this comment:

> *"Even though they face the awesome power of the White House and the daily danger of Obama's veto pen, Republicans must heed John F. Kennedy's exhortation to "pay any price, bear any burden, meet any hardship, support any friend, oppose any foe, in order to assure the survival and the success of liberty" and to preserve, protect and defend America."*

Any conservative who gives something to liberals to gain something else just kissed away the future. And that conservative needs to be removed from office. When negotiating with liberals, gridlock is better than compromises that lose ground. What did Churchill say? "Never give in—never, never, never, never, in nothing great or small, large or petty, never give in except to convictions of honor and good sense."

Compromise must be used selfishly. Any compromise must advance the conservative cause or compromise should not be used. Any compromise that moves the current state closer to what is desired by liberals should automatically be rejected by conservatives.

In summary, to fight this war against liberal radicals, conservatives need to: *Save, Challenge , Talk the talk, Walk the walk*, and *Compromise selfishly*.

These are verbs. They are actions.

Now let me add one more thing. George W. Bush used the term "compassionate conservative."

Conservatives are compassionate. Conservatives voluntarily donate more time and more money to their churches, to needy organizations, and to world causes than liberals ever do. Conservatives give voluntary donations of their own resources. Charity. Compassion. Self sacrifice.

Compare that to the liberals who take money from others as taxes and then give it to those who vote for them. There is no self-sacrifice in taking from some and then giving it to others. No charity. No compassion. That is theft.

The issue is not compassion. Conservatives have always had compassion. The issue is passion. Passion makes things happen. Tea party participants showed passion and they made a difference.

Just think what would happen if all conservatives became "passionate conservatives?"

To defeat evil will require "passionate conservatives." It will require good men and women who will "take action" so that evil will not triumph.

Chapter 5
Guns

The Second Amendment to the Constitution of the United States says:

> *... the right of the people to keep and bear Arms, shall not be infringed.*

How can the intent of the Founding Fathers be any clearer? The local and federal governments in the USA cannot infringe on the right of the people to keep and bear arms.

Yet, liberals continually try to ban guns.

Totalitarian governments ban weapons in the civilian population so that the government is the only one with weapons.

In two separate cases within the last couple of years, all four of the Supreme Court Justices who are considered to be liberals voted against the ownership of guns by the general population while all four of the Supreme Court Justices who are considered to be conservative voted that the Second Amendment allows citizens to own guns.

The moderate Supreme Court Justice sided with the conservatives, so interpretation of the Constitution is now set that citizens can own guns. What would happen if one of those

Supreme Court conservatives or moderates were to leave the court and a liberal was appointed to replace the conservative/moderate? Do you think for a moment that the new court would hesitate to hear a new case that would negate the established interpretation?

If "activist" judges can interpret "the right of the people to keep and bear Arms, shall not be infringed" to mean something other than what those words actually state, then what else in the Constitution is being interpreted to mean something other than what the words actually state?

Activist judges have already ruled deliberately against the 10th Amendment to allow the Federal Government more authority than what the 10th Amendment allows. The 10th Amendment clearly states… *The powers not delegated to the United States by the Constitution, nor prohibited by it to the States, are reserved to the States respectively, or to the people.*

So why is the right to own guns under the Second Amendment so important? Because if the courts can abuse the Second Amendment with activist interpretations when the Second Amendment is so clearly stated, then the courts can abuse any part of the Constitution. The way a judge interprets the Second Amendment is the litmus test about how that judge will treat the rest of the Constitution, especially the Tenth Amendment. And liberal judges continually find ways to interpret the Second Amendment with activist rulings that are totally different than what it says. So what else are they interpreting differently than what the Constitution actually says?

A couple of liberal congressional representatives stated that there is no reason for anyone to own assault weapons because they are not allowed for hunting. Once again, the liberals are trying to redefine gun ownership—this time by defining ownership of guns to be for hunting so that they might ban certain types of ownership that are used for purposes other than hunting.

Where are their heads? Citizens are allowed to own guns to defend themselves; not just for hunting. There is nothing in the Second Amendment that limits gun ownership to hunting.

So what else are the liberals doing? Hillary Clinton certainly did not accept the Supreme Court rulings. She is trying to enter into treaties with foreign nations that include gun bans so that those treaties will negate our own Constitution.

The Common Sense Gun Lobby sent out a letter on December 1, 2010. It has been edited so that the most important parts of its message are included:

Patriotic American, Barack Hussein Obama is determined to see the proposed UN Small Arms Treaty ratified...

... when people hear it, most of them shrug because they believe the 2nd Amendment will prevent its implementation in the United States. That's wrong thinking because the moment you ignore any threat that threatens your security, the threat becomes reality...

... When Mr. Obama moves on this treaty, he will still control the U.S. Senate which is the only body that votes on ratification. If ratified, the UN Small Arms Treaty could do the following:

1. *It could require U. S. citizens to deliver any banned firearms they own to the local government "collection and destruction center"—or face imprisonment. It could prohibit any transfer of firearm ownership.*

2. It could require the destruction of "excess" firearms.

3. It could prohibit firearm and ammunition manufacturers from selling to the public.

4. It could require micro-stamping on all guns.

If you think, "Nah, that can't happen here. We're protected by the 2nd Amendment." Think again. The United Nations Small Arms Trade Treaty ... would be a United Nations Treaty ... Obama Administration is trying to "back door" the American people by erasing the most basic American right in the Constitution via a United Nations' treaty that would abrogate the 2nd Amendment.

... Like they did with Obamacare, the anti-gun proponents... are plotting how to ram this treaty down our throats. The Obama administration is "hell-bent" to take away your guns, so they can continue to expand their absolute control over the American people. If the treaty is ever ratified, the abuse from our own federal government will obsessively increase.

This is not a fight about gun ownership. It is a fight about our Constitution. It is a fight about our rights as stated in the Bill of Rights. It is a fight about literal interpretation of words versus an activist interpretation of words.

Article V of the Constitution stipulates how the Constitution and its amendments are to be amended. The amendment process in Article V is part of the contract of the Constitution between "we the people" and our government. Activist judges and liberal lawyers continually look for ways to circumvent the Constitution. Activist interpretations and treaties are methods used to play games with the Constitution so the process of Article V can be ignored. And if the government can get away with negating the Second Amendment without using Article V to amend it, then liberals can play games with anything else in the Constitution.

Guns are important in America because they represent all of the terms in the Constitution. Gun ownership is the symbol of all the rights established as part of our Bill of Rights in the Constitution. As liberals try to circumvent the process of Article V for changing the Second Amendment about gun ownership, they destroy the Constitution as a contract between "we the people" and our federal government.

Save. The fight about gun ownership is a fight about maintaining our Constitution as the contract that limits the powers of government and how that contract can be amended. Every conservative needs to join this fight to save our rights, save our Constitution, and save America.

Do you own a gun? Not me. But the right to own a gun needs to be defended diligently by every conservative. Gun ownership is a symbol of all of our rights. As the right to own guns is diminished without the due process of amendment in Article V, so can all the other aspects of the Constitution be diminished by acts of circumvention of the limits placed on the federal government in the Constitution.

Challenge. The argument used by liberals to ban guns is that guns kill people and that bad guys use guns to do bad things.

Conservatives need to challenge liberals about this basic premise:

- If guns are banned, will bad guys give up ownership of their guns? No. So then only bad guys will own guns. So how will good people defend themselves from bad guys?

- Do guns kill or do people kill? So why penalize all the law abiding people because of the bad people?

- OK, if guns are so bad, then why don't liberals propose an amendment to the Constitution to ban them? Why do liberals continually try to ban them with surreptitious actions?

Bad guys in Congress also use the legislative process to do bad things ... so should we ban Congress?

Talk the Talk. Speak up. Tell your Congressman how you feel. The toll free number for your Congressman is readily available: 1-800-227-2477. Use it. Tell your friends how you feel. Explain to your children why the right to own a gun is so important.

At a dinner some time ago, an executive friend of mine was entertaining his young staff. He spoke about how he loved to go to the shooting range and practice shooting. The faces on his staff showed disbelief. The jaw on one young lady actually dropped. There was horror in her eyes. She asked him how could he do that? The executive answered that he enjoyed it, that guns were an American right not granted in totalitarian run countries, and that he did it because so many in government don't want him to do it.

Then when one of his staff asked him if he owned any guns, he answered "Yes, 8 guns... a shotgun, an AR-15 rifle, a hunting rifle, and 5 handguns." Those young people were aghast. They were taught by the government run education system that only people in West Virginia and bad guys owned guns.

One of the young staffers asked him why he owned guns? And he answered, "Because in America, I can."

That was the first time that those young staff people had ever encountered anyone who actually owned guns. To find out that someone who was their leader, a college educated executive, owned guns was a moment of awakening for them. It was counter to what they had been taught in school and on TV.

If the executive had not talked about this, then those young people might have continued to believe that the only ones who own guns are bad guys and/or people who live in the back woods as the liberals had them believing.

He talked the talk.

Walk the Walk. Conservatives need to support those organizations that support gun ownership. And conservatives need to vote for politicians who will protect the Second Amendment unless it is changed by the proper process as defined in Article V.

Join the NRA (National Rifle Association). Call 1-703-267-1000.

The NRA will send you a cool hat that has NRA on it. When you wear that hat, you will discover friends that you never knew existed. Your hand will get raw from all the high fives that you will get. Hot women love guys in the NRA hat. And men love hot women who wear the NRA hat. Just wearing the NRA hat will demonstrate everything that needs to be demonstrated about your feelings about gun ownership rights. You will be walking the walk when you wear an NRA hat.

The NRA works to protect the Second Amendment. They will keep you posted about treaties, activist judgments, and other activities that are designed to dilute the right of gun ownership. Periodically, the NRA will ask you to make phone calls or send FAX messages or sign petitions to stop actions that harm the Second Amendment without the due process of amending it under Article V.

The NRA will get you to walk the walk.

By joining the NRA, the NRA can then claim one more person who agrees with them about Second Amendment rights as the NRA lobbies Congress. It is hard for a politician to ignore millions of people watching his/her actions toward the Second Amendment as part of the NRA.

And the NRA will periodically send you videos and magazines with some of the coolest weapons in the world.

Walk the walk so that the "right of the people to keep and bear Arms" shall not be infringed.

Compromise Selfishly. There is no compromise about gun ownership that does not harm the conservative position.

Ban ammunition? No, that will just create a black market that caters to bad guys as it reduces the ability of citizens to defend themselves. Banning ammunition is the same as banning guns. How does a citizen defend self, family, or property if there is no ammunition?

Raise taxes on ammunition? No, bad guys will still buy ammunition. And raising taxes, any taxes, is a bad thing for conservatives.

OK, maybe a case can be made that ownership of tanks and surface to air missiles should be excluded as part of the rights in the Second Amendment. But certainly, there is no compromise about rifles and handguns that does not diminish the rights of citizens to defend themselves.

Chapter 6
Religion

The First Amendment to the Constitution of the United States says:

> *Congress shall make no law respecting an establishment of religion, or prohibiting the free exercise thereof; or abridging the freedom of speech, or of the press; or the right of the people peaceably to assemble, and to petition the Government for a redress of grievances.*

The limitation in regards to religion is that "Congress shall make no law respecting the establishment of religion..."—nothing more and nothing less. And Congress cannot pass any laws "prohibiting the free exercise thereof ..."

There are no limitations on religious organizations and none on individuals as to how and where they express their religions—including in government owned buildings. So how does the Supreme Court justify its actions of prohibiting the free exercise of religion in schools or other public settings? How does our Supreme Court justify its actions of limiting the free speech of religious leaders about political issues when the Constitution clearly states, "Congress shall make no law... abridging the freedom of speech?"

There is nothing in the First Amendment that allows our Supreme Court to do what it has done concerning the limitations on religious freedom of speech and actions. How can the Congress pass laws that deny non-profit status to religious organizations if they promote a political candidate? What is in the Constitution that grants Congress such authority? The Constitution clearly states, "Congress shall make no law... abridging the freedom of speech?"

The First Amendment simply says that "Congress shall make no laws..."

Nothing else.

The Holy Cross Catholic Church in Kingston, Jamaica is a very humble church. Its parishioners are mostly poor compared to USA standards. Its parishioners are practically all black. It collects all of its own funds to help the less fortunate and to fund its many community projects. It has a congregational prayer that reads in part:

> *Father, before your Son returned to You. He commanded His followers to "Go and make disciples of all nations." Empowered by the Holy Spirit, the disciples relentlessly preached the Good News, and paved the way for us to receive Christ and become his followers... that we may feel compelled to "Doing the Work Of The One Who Sent Me" with courage and boldness, fearing no one, but you.*

Our Founding Fathers passed the First Amendment of the Constitution to allow any and all disciples of any and all religions to "do the work of the one who sent them" without restriction by government of any kind as long as their actions do not harm others. And harm is limited to those acts of physical, political, and monetary harm—unlike the claims of the ACLU that Christians harm others psychologically by just celebrating Christmas in public. The Founding Fathers used the terms of "God" and "creator" and "created' in our Declaration of Independence and Constitution.

Activist judges with a mission to destroy the influence of Christians on America used a definition of separation of church and state that is outside of the Constitution. Thomas Jefferson's opinion was that there needed to be a separation of church and state. He expressed his view after the Constitution was ratified. He was not even the author of the Constitution. He wrote his opinion in a letter to explain why the "government" should not establish a church like the British government did. Therefore, he suggested that there is "a wall of separation between the church and state" in the U.S.

Nowhere in the Constitution of the United States is the term "separation of church and state" used. It was a deliberate omission by the authors and signers of the Constitution. It is not an agreed term in the contract between we the people and our federal government. It is outside of the four corners of the Constitution.

Liberals use the Jefferson opinion as a fact of the Constitution. Some activist judges have reached outside of the four corners of the Constitution to use it as the law—when it is not. The Constitution simply says that the "Congress shall make no laws" concerning an establishment of a government run church and/ or concerning any restrictions on exercising religious beliefs. Activist judges have once again usurped the rights of "we the people" in the Constitution which requires that any changes to it be made by the amendment process of Article V. They changed the Constitution by using terms from outside of the Constitution and by a secularist interpretation of those terms.

In addition, those judges usurped the rights of the states in the Tenth Amendment. States can establish religious preference. They can establish a state run church. There is nothing in the Constitution that forbids them from such acts. The only restriction concerning religion and government is that "Congress shall make no laws." The federal courts have once again overstepped their authorities to promote a liberal secularist agenda. And then they set themselves up as the "court of last resort."

Well, they are wrong. As stated in the Declaration of Independence, the court of last resort rests with "we the people":

> *whenever any form of government becomes destructive of these ends, it is the right of the people to alter or to abolish it, and to institute new government.*

The true fact is this: liberals not only want a separation of church and state. Liberals want the state to replace religion as the keeper of values.

The following is an excerpt from an article written by Jon Christian Ryter titled "Erasing Christianity":

> *We could argue that the contemporary assault on Christianity began with a little-noticed brochure from the American Bar Association [ABA to its members] in May, 1989, advertising a seminar for "...[a]ttorneys who want to be on the leading edge of an explosive new area of law"—suing churches, Christian leaders and Christian activists. The seminar was*

entitled: "Expanding Use of Tort Law Against Religions." While this would trigger a new phase of attacks on Christianity, in reality, the assault on the Christian Church was launched shortly after the end of World War II with the birth of the United Nations and the reemergence of the globalist movement that lay dormant for two decades.

... It became very clear to the globalists between the two world wars that, before American sovereignty could be breached the utopians—aided by corrupt political hacks, judges, and bureaucrats—would have to erase Christianity from the hearts, minds and souls of the American people before the United States could be re-shackled to the Old World Order. The utopians would attack the underpinnings of the 1st Amendment. They knew if they could erode the right of free men to speak on the issues that affected their lives, or prevent those free men from expressing their religious beliefs, they would no longer be free...

... 1946. That year the attitude of the federal courts changed. The restriction placed in the 1st Amendment by the Founding Fathers against their newly formed government— "Congress shall make no law respecting the establishment of religion, or prohibiting the free exercise thereof..."—would be shifted by activist federal judges away from the government and used against the people whose right to worship without restrictions could not be constitutionally abridged by the government or the courts....

In order to begin erasing the generational isolationism that had permeated America since WWI, President **Harry S. Truman** *introduced a UN public school curriculum created by UNESCO into the American school system on April 6,*

1946. The curriculum, "Towards World Understanding" was designed to prepare America's next generations for "world citizenship." The following year UNESCO's Director General, **Sir Julian Huxley,** *issued a scholastic directive entitled "Classrooms With Children Under 12-years of Age" which blamed the parents of school children for harming their offspring by instilling in them a sense of Christian faith and patriotic pride.* **Huxley** *said that "...[b]efore the child enters school his mind has already been profoundly marked, and often injuriously, by earlier influences...first gained...in the home." Later in the text—which was used in hundreds of classrooms throughout the nation—* **Huxley** *observed "... it is frequently the family that infects the child with extreme nationalism. The school should therefore use the means described earlier to combat family attitudes." Among those things that "infect" the family,* **Huxley** *reiterated again, were religion and patriotism.*

Huxley's *utopian UN programs were incorporated in the public school system of the United States and eventually became the foundational framework for preschool—getting the children away from their parents before they are unduly influenced by homegrown parental prejudices—God and country. Today, a half-century later, the American family has come to believe that preschool is good for their children and that it's also good for them. They believe that by getting their kids into school earlier, the children learn faster, and learn more. Nothing could be farther from the truth. As was proven by* **Dr. James Dobson** *three decades ago, children not only learn faster, but they retained much more of what they learn if they are held out of school until age seven.*

The government, through its Congressional incorporation—the National Education Association—is merely exercising the Huxley Principle by encouraging parents to place their children in preschool classes and even curriculurized daycare. Get the children away from their parents and surrender them to the "Village" as soon as possible. No God. No country. No homegrown prejudices to interfere with the New World Order brainwashing. One government. One economy. One religion—the State. **Huxley's** *anti-Christian principles, carefully woven into the public school curriculum through UNESCO launched a generational attack on Christianity not only in the United States but around the world.*

From 1946 until 1965 the battle was waged almost entirely from within the citadels of public education as the American Civil Liberties Union was drafted by the utopians in the American Bar Association to carry the separation of church and state banner in the battle against God in the courtrooms...

It's important to stop and examine the inherent ideology of the court that declared war on religion in America. It was a mirror reflection of the very first Supreme Court—philosophically opposite of the views of the high court justices picked by **George Washington.** *The first US Supreme Court contained five justices:* **John Jay, John Rutledge, William Cushing, Robert Harrison, James Wilson** *and* **John Blair.** *While all of them were Federalists, each understood that the Constitution not only prevented any legislative body in the land from restricting the right of the people to worship, it also prevented any court in the land—the Supreme Court as well—from restricting or abridging that right.*

The First Amendment was a safeguard designed specifically to prevent the federal government from creating a state-sponsored religion, or from interfering with the rights of the people to worship God as they saw fit when, where, and how, they wanted. The New Deal Court that heard Everson was appointed almost exclusively by **Franklin D. Roosevelt.** *Its justices were largely social activists who had signed on to the* **Roosevelt** *agenda. And topping FDR's agenda was converting the League of Nations into the United Nations— and creating world government.* **Roosevelt,** *like most of the world's leaders, believed that establishing world government was the only way to prevent war. Believing the adult generations of the world had too many homegrown prejudices to live war-free, the UN concentrated on indoctrinating the children of the world—the next generation of adults—to live together in peace. The agent of change would be UNESCO.*

The New Deal Court contained seven justices picked by **FDR: Wiley Rutledge, Frank Murphy, Robert Jackson, Felix Frankfurter, Hugo Black, Stanley Reed** *and* **William O. Douglas.** *Each of these justices were appointed specifically because they were utopian liberals who very specifically and very privately agreed to protect* **FDR's** *unconstitutional New Deal laws. The remaining two members of the New Deal Court were appointed by* **Harry S. Truman** *who, as vice president, ascended to the presidency upon the death of* **FDR** *in April 1945. They were* **Fred Vinson,** *appointed as Chief Justice, and* **Harold Burton. Washington** *and* **FDR** *were the only two presidents who appointed majority opinion courts which virtually rubber-stamped their agendas by guaranteeing they would be upheld if challenged in the federal courts.*

The liberal establishment has unilaterally controlled the philosophical slant of the U.S. Supreme Court since 1937...

As long as the liberals control the Supreme Court, the attack against Christianity will continue in the United States. *If a major philosophical change on the high court does not happen soon, religious liberty will be legislatively abolished and Christianity will be branded as an exclusive, rather than inclusive, racist religion, justifying the "Village" in erasing it from the American society. It was because of the deliberate politicizing of the high court that the virulent attack on Christianity was allowed to happen, and why it is tolerated by the judiciary.*

The liberal judiciary in the United States will completely erase the tenets of Christianity from the land by successfully branding it a racist religion, and allowing civil rights groups to sue it out of existence.

This article points out so many abuses. First of all, federal judges are political. They are part of the federal government and are appointed by the executive branch. Federal judges have the political agenda of the president or they would not get appointed. They are no longer part of the intended system of checks and balance that our founding fathers created. Next, Christianity is under attack because it is in direct opposition to the liberal agenda of a New World Order—especially their objective to reduce the world population substantially. And last, liberals and activist judges are using the school system of the USA to brainwash our children—the next generation of Americans—to accept the liberal goal of a secularist state. As stated in *Save America Now*, tyrants do not want a free religious society. Tyrants want to control values in the society. Religious based values present competition to the imposed values of tyrants. Religions present other viewpoints which might disagree with the tyrants' views.

Therefore, tyrants will either make the government be the religious head like in Iran and other Muslim countries and Great Britain in the 1770s, or they will outlaw public religious practice and impose a secular society like in Communist countries.

The First Amendment of the U.S. Constitution is a threat to tyrants. It is a threat to liberals who want to control the values in America.

As the federal government gets closer to imposing a complete secular society in the USA, it is violating the First Amendment in the Constitution without the due process of amendment in Article V of the Constitution. The government is sponsoring the establishment of secularist religious beliefs. And when the government limits the practice of Christianity, it violates the First Amendment by prohibiting the free exercise thereof and freedom of speech and freedom of assembly.

This U.S. government has gone so far as to alter history, continually. The day after the Japanese bombed Pearl Harbor, President Roosevelt said these words during a speech to America:

Yesterday, December 7, 1941—a date which will live in infamy—the United States of America was suddenly and deliberately attacked. With confidence in our armed forces, with the abounding determination of our people, we will gain the inevitable triumph, so help us God.

At the memorial to the soldiers of WWII in Washington, DC, those last four words "so help us God" were omitted. Barack Hussein Obama has done this several times when referencing the Declaration of Independence. He omits "God" and "creator." How many more textbooks, quotations, and legal interpretations have been altered to fit the liberal secularist agenda?

Read the First Amendment again: *Congress shall make no law respecting an establishment of religion, or prohibiting the free exercise thereof;*

Secularism, atheism, and agnosticism are religious beliefs. The government can make no law establishing them. And the government cannot prohibit the free exercise of Christianity—anywhere and at any time.

Rather than protecting the Constitution, our government, the judicial branch is violating it.

In addition, the government allows those who dismiss Christian values to continually corrupt America. Paul, an Apostle of Jesus, was very clear that this would happen as part of the plan of the devil when he stated in II Timothy 4: "For the time is coming when people will no longer listen to the right teaching of sound doctrine. They will follow their own desires and will look for teachers to tickle their ears by telling them what they want to hear."

Corruption of values is the easy way. Give people what they want to hear rather than what they need to hear. Dr. Gregory Thomson writes in *Giving Aid and Comfort to the Enemy* that "America, once a strong Christian nation, was a beacon of light to the world, but has been infiltrated by traitors against God, family, and nation. This enemy that is within is rotting the nation internally..." Let me add that it is deliberate and that the courts are complicit. They are deliberately moving America away from Judeo/Christian based values in favor of an erosion of values. And they are deliberately negating the First Amendment with overreaching activist interpretations of the Constitution to do it.

John 5:36: "Doing the work of the one who sent me."

It is my opinion that all people do the work of the one who sent them. And you can tell who sent them by the work that they do. Who would send someone to encourage abortion? Who would send those who limit the free speech of Christians? Who would send someone to strike God and religion from USA history books and from classrooms? Who would send those who demine the sanctity of marriage between and man and a woman? Who would send someone to steal money in the form of taxes by the government and then give that money to Planned Parenthood for sponsoring abortions, or to unions who oppose the right of individuals to work without union representation, or to foreign countries that kill Christians? Who would send those judges who allow all of this to happen?

Whoever sent them must be very evil.

So what should conservatives do to stop this erosion of the First Amendment by liberals? What should each of us do to protect the right to practice religion at any time and any place? What should be done to stop those who have been sent by the evil one?

Save. Oh, who can save our heritage? Who can save our Constitution? Who can save God as part of our history?

The words of the Founding Fathers were filled with inspiration from God. Our Declaration of Independence glorifies God, the creator. So who can save our heritage when so many are trying to eliminate God from our heritage?

G. Henkel, a spiritual advisor, points out, "God is Omnipresent which means God is everywhere and in everything, including us. Sit by the ocean, take a walk in nature, hold a baby, talk to a small child or just be still, fill your mind with love and peaceful thoughts, and you will feel God right there." Our forefathers knew this. To deny the influence of God on our forefathers is deceit.

Even if you do not believe in God, do you believe in our Constitution? Then do you understand that any actions by our government to establish a secularist society establishes a government sponsored religion of secularism and it prohibits the free exercise of other religions? Do you understand that the government is doing this without the due process for amendment to our Constitution that is stated in Article V?

To save our constitution, conservatives need to save the First Amendment as it is written and not as some activist judges interpret it. Read the words. What do they say to you?

Congress shall make no law respecting an establishment of religion, or prohibiting the free exercise thereof;

There is nothing in the First Amendment that restricts the exercise of any religion at any location at any time. Those judges who outlaw the expressions of faith from public or private locations have overstepped their authorities. The only restriction mentioned in the Constitution is that "Congress" shall make no "law" respecting an establishment of religion... and "Congress" shall make no "law" prohibiting the free exercise thereof (religion). Nowhere is there any statement about how any exercise of religion is prohibited in any way—in public locations or in private locations.

There is nothing in the Constitution that prohibits any state or other local government from promoting any religion that it wants to promote. To the contrary, the Tenth Amendment states that since the federal Congress is barred from passing any laws of any kind that pertain to establishment or restriction of religion, then that function clearly belongs to the states and/or the people.

Activist judges have modified our Constitution without a mandate from "we the people" as stipulated in Article V. Those judges are traitors to the country governed by the Constitution as per Article III, Section 3 and to their oath to protect and defend the Constitution.

This example of how judges are overstepping their authority about religion is repeated over and over about many other topics such as mandated healthcare "insurance" as part of Interstate Commerce and the monopolistic control of labor resources by unions without regulation by the government. They do it with interpretation of "standing" so that we the people have no individual "standing" to enforce our Constitution about the natural born citizenship of Barack Hussein Obama. Etc., etc. Judges are political. They practice political bias.

Do you understand how activist judges are destroying our Constitution and that it needs to be saved? Do you understand how liberals in charge of our schools and textbooks are methodically eliminating God from our history?

We need to save America from activist judges. We need to save the religious aspects of American history from the liberal history revisionists.

The first step is to save God as part of our heritage. Anything else is condoning the lie that God, religion, had no part in the establishment of America. Conservatives need to save God in our heritage, enforce the First Amendment as it is written, to help save America as a republic governed by a constitution.

Challenge. In his booklet, *Voting with a Clear Conscience*, Reverend Frank Pavone, the National Director of the Gospel of Life, states: "Most disagreements between candidates and political platforms do not have to do with *principle*, but rather with *policy*." He continues, "As long as the policy doesn't break the principle, both policies may well be morally legitimate. It remains to be seen by trial and error, which works best. But when a policy dispute involves questioning whether people deserve that (item) in the first place, that policy is the principle."

Today, the actions of liberals signal that they do not believe in the principle of freedom of religion. All of their actions to limit the stated rights to practice religion and to limit religious freedom of speech are morally illegitimate as they attack the basic principle of freedom of religion in our Constitution.

Reverend Pavone used this example to make his point: "It is a basic principle that people have a right to safety of their own lives and possessions. That's why we have to fight crime. We don't see campaigning on opposite sides of that principle, with some saying, "Fight Crime" and others defending "The Right to Crime." Instead, there is an agreement in the principle, but disagreement on the best policies to implement the principle."

Using Reverend Pavone's logic, liberals are not in agreement with the principles in the First and Tenth Amendments of the Constitution. Their policies usurp it. They do not believe in freedom of religion. They do not believe that religious organizations can practice unrestricted freedom of speech. And they do not believe that *The powers not delegated to the United States by the Constitution, nor prohibited by it to the States, are reserved to the States respectively, or to the people,* as stated in the Tenth Amendment.

This is a disagreement of principle—not one of policy.

It is time to challenge our courts. It is time to ask the hard questions of every federal judicial candidate and every active federal judge:

- Is it OK for you go outside of the four corners of our Constitution and its amendments to formulate judicial opinions?

- Is separation of church and state a Constitutional term?

- Can the federal government limit exercising freedom of religion in any way if that exercise does not threaten the physical well being of others?

- Are religious representatives/organizations restricted from having the same rights of freedom of speech as does anyone else?

If a federal judicial candidate or judge answers "yes" to any of those questions, then that candidate and/or judge is not qualified to be a federal judge because that candidate and/or judge does not agree with the principles of the very Constitution that he or she is supposed to "defend and protect."

This is not about political policies. It is about "defending and protecting" the principles in our constitution.

The same is true about education, media, entertainment, and all those who influence others. Every time they mention how separation of church and state is the law of the land, they need to be challenged. Those same four questions need to be asked of each of them whenever they try to use "separation of church and state" as justification for government sanctioned secularism.

Conservatives need to challenge the slow encroachment of the words protecting freedom of religion in our Constitution. So often, cases are taken into courts by the ACLU or others who claim that some Christian expression of faith offends them; and many courts side with them. Challenge that. Doesn't their attack on the basic principles of religious freedom, of freedom of speech, and of state's rights offend you? Challenge them.

Talk the Talk. The last major polls by Pew, Gallup, Zogby, and Rasmussen show that somewhere between 70 and 80 percent of Americans are Christians. So why do so many institutions enforce a "Happy Holidays" code instead of "Merry Christmas?" Who are the bosses? Who is making those decisions?

So do you say "Merry Christmas?" Or do you say "Happy Holidays" to be politically correct?

Our Declaration of Independence for the United States says that all men are "created equal" with the rights of *life, liberty, and the pursuit of happiness.*

Hmm. So when does that "creation" take place? Is it at conception? If so, then why don't you speak up against abortion?

Why don't you speak up in defense of religious rights? How can the federal government demand that religious sponsored hospitals perform abortions? Abortion funding is hidden in Obamacare as part of funding for organizations that condone abortion.

Since the Founding Fathers were clear that our rights are from God, then why isn't everyone speaking up in defense of the impact of God and religion on the history and heritage of America? Why are we allowing history revisionists to remove reference to God? Why are we allowing Obama to drop "creator" from his quotes of the Declaration of Independence without any criticism of his actions?

Conservative silence empowers liberals. Saul Alinsky instructed liberals to silence conservatives. And if conservatives remain silent, then liberals will change the rights that are gifts of God and the principles established in our Constitution without ever having to bring such actions to a vote of the American public or a vote of our representatives. They will negate the safe guard against such actions that is established as the amendment process established in Article V of the Constitution.

Speak up. Talk the talk. Are you a Christian? Are you Jewish? Do you believe in religious freedom, in the freedom of speech, and in state's rights? Well then, speak up!

Walk the Walk. Do you believe that it is a mother's right to chose to kill her unborn child or not? For women: have you had an abortion? For men: did you allow an abortion to happen?

Reverend Frank Pavone's *Voting with a Clear Conscience* cites Mother Theresa of Calcutta:

The greatest destroyer of peace is abortion... Many people are very, very concerned with the children of India, with the children of Africa where quite a number die, maybe of malnutrition, of hunger and so on, but many are dying deliberately by the will of the mother. And this is what is the greatest destroyer of peace today. Because if a mother can kill her own child, what is left for me to kill you and you to kill me? There is nothing in between.

The New World Order and its liberal supporters really do want to reduce the world population. They cannot do it as long as religious principles state that the unborn child is alive. They cannot do it as long as religious principles state that abortion is murder. So they are deliberately working to reduce the influence of religion, especially Christianity, on society.

So will you let this happen?

Today, it is time to impeach all those judges who use an activist approach to their judicial decisions. It is time to stop the appointment of judges who erode the words in our Constitution by liberal interpretations. It is time to inspect closely what is being taught to our children about religion and about abortion and then fire those educators who teach our children things that we do not want taught. It is time to walk the walk.

We as mankind cannot legislate away the rules of God. If you are a Christian, you cannot justify abortion because the rules of man say it is okay. God's laws trump man's laws. Otherwise, concepts like being "created equally with the rights of life, liberty, and the pursuit of happiness" will be at risk as man's laws will be allowed to trump God's laws.

It is time to walk the walk.

We have all done things that are wrong in the eyes of God. We cannot legislate those things into being okay. We cannot deem them to be okay by becoming a secularist society. We cannot change the definitions of right and wrong by stopping the practice of religion and becoming a secularist society.

God either exists or does not. Legislation by man will not change the fact of God's existence or not. And legislation by man cannot change what is right and wrong in the eyes of God.

This is the biggest difference between liberals and conservatives. Liberals believe that man can change God's laws while conservatives do not. Murder is murder even if man's laws sanction it—and that includes abortion. Theft is theft even if it is sanctioned by the government as "redistribution of wealth" or as "social justice." Envy is an act of "coveting" even if it is promoted by politicians in class warfare for political power.

The Liberty Council (Liberty University School of Law) walks the walk. It is not afraid of losing its tax-exempt status to speak up for religious freedom and Christian values in politics as so many Catholic churches will not.

The American Civil Liberties Union (ACLU) used the Saul Alinsky playbook to threaten Christianity out of schools. The ACLU uses intimidation to promote the New World Order plan of secularism. Public schools and the Catholic Church are so frightened about being dragged into court cases by the ACLU that they capitulate to it continuously when in fact the ACLU is wrong. During the Christmas season in 2010, the ACLU sent letters to the public school executives in Tennessee instructing them that displays and demonstrations of Christianity would be considered to be unconstitutional. The ACLU would consider such acts as promotion of the Christian faith by a government organization.

All too often, this type of intimidation by the ACLU worked—but not this time. The Liberty Council countered the ACLU with letters to the school executives in Tennessee and the rest of the USA. The Liberty Council cited the ruling of the Supreme Court in 1984 that said that public display and demonstration of Christianity was sanctioned as freedom of religion as long as other religious beliefs and/or secular beliefs were not deliberately excluded. The Liberty Council is the real hero riding on a white horse and wearing a white hat for all those groups who fear the ACLU. The Liberty Council fights the ACLU in and out of court and wins. The Liberty Council fights for rights of religious groups to participate in politics and to practice religious beliefs at any time and at any place as part of freedom of religion and freedom of speech as guaranteed in the First Amendment of the Constitution.

The Liberty Council walks the walk.

If you are Christian or Jewish, then:

- It is impossible for you to vote for secularist politicians without betraying your faith.

- It is impossible for you to support the ACLU without betraying your faith.

- It is impossible for you to allow an activist interpretation of our Constitution without betraying your faith.

- It is impossible for you to vote for those who sanction abortion without betraying your faith.

- It is impossible for you to approve of legislation that sanctions abortion like Obamacare without betraying your faith.

So it is time to walk the walk. It is time for each of us to get down on our knees and ask God to forgive us. God knows that we humans are not perfect. God simply asks us to repent and try a little harder. God asks each of us to love each other, love life from conception to death, and try a little harder to be God's children.

It is time for each of us to walk the walk. It is time for each of us to do the work of the one who sent us.

Compromise Selfishly. The differences between the liberal and the conservative approaches to freedom of religion and of religious free speech are ones of principle, and not ones of policy. They cannot be reconciled.

Legislation of policy items like passing Obamacare with imbedded funding for abortions in them are compromises to principle. And those compromises to religious principle cannot be reconciled. They cannot be justified.

On a church sponsored mission to Jamaica in March 2011, one of the high schools in Jamaica sponsored by our church had a debate about abortion. One of the debate teams represented the anti-abortion view and another team represented the right to choose an abortion view. All of the students were assembled for it. The anti-abortion team won the debate as per a vote of the students after the anti-abortion team made these arguments:

> *"If creation begins with conception, then how can abortion of that creation be anything other than murder?"*
>
> *"How can the fetus be considered to be part of the body of the mother when it is a different person—different DNA, different blood, etc.—inside of that mother? The mother is a carrier for the child—connected by an umbilical cord—but they are different people, so how can anyone consider the*

unborn child to be the part of the body of the mother for her to kill if she wishes to do so?"

Now let me ask this: How is it that these students in Jamaica understand these simple arguments and so many Americans do not? Could it be because so many Americans do not want to accept what is so obvious? The fetus is a different person from the mother. The question of abortion is not about the mother's body. It is about the life of the fetus. It is about these words from our Founding Fathers: *That all men are created equal; that they are endowed by their Creator with certain unalienable rights; that among these are life, liberty, and the pursuit of happiness.*

Creation happens at the time of conception by God, the Creator.

Joe Sestak was the Democrat Congressman from Pennsylvania who led the Democrat revolt against Obamacare because of funding for abortions that was imbedded in the legislation. Joe wanted to help the less fortunate with government funded healthcare, but understood that funding abortions was too much of a violation to Christian principle to allow him to vote for Obamacare.

We compassionate Americans might want to help those who are less fortunate with programs like free healthcare to those in economic need. But if we allow our compassion to be used to also grant funding for other things that are principally wrong like with abortion or with mandatory "insurance," then that compromise affects basic established principles and not just policy. Therefore, there is no acceptable compromise.

Eventually, Joe Sestak succumbed to the political pressure from the Democrat Party and he voted against his own conscience and voted for Obamacare. Joe Sestak violated principle in favor of policy. He was wrong. What compromise could have allowed his conscience to violate such basic principle?

Joe Sestack claimed that Barack Hussein Obama promised him that funding for groups who condone abortions would be removed from the legislation by executive order and stated that the USA needed Obamacare because it would decrease insurance costs and the deficit.

Joe Sestack knew—or should have known as a legislator—that the promise from Obama was a lie. In the *Washington Times* of March 21, 2010, Betsy McCaughey, former lieutenant governor of New York, said:

> *President Barack Obama is trying to lure anti-abortion Democrats to vote yes for the Senate health bill with promises that he will "fix" their fears of abortion funding with an Executive Order. But Executive Orders cannot change the law. The Supreme Court made that clear in Youngstown Sheet & Tube Company v. Sawyer, 33 US 579 (1952).*

A year after passage of Obamacare, the executive order had no effect on Obamacare since it was a law of Congress and signed by the president without changes. Insurance costs have increased, abortions are funded, and the OMB revised its estimate and now says that Obamacare will increase the deficit.

Sestak used the promise from Obama as an excuse to vote for Obamacare and violated his principles. He deceived his constituents, and violated their trust. Obama deceived

America by promising to issue an executive order that he knew would be invalid.

Joe Sestak violated his principles.

As for politicians, as stated by Reverend Pavone: "(We must) disqualify (ed) those candidates who violate fundamental principles."

While there might be acceptable compromises to policy, there can be no compromises to fundamental principles of freedom of religion, of freedom of speech, of states' rights to promote religions as they choose, and of the right to life at creation, *conception*—"created" with the rights of life, liberty, and the pursuit of happiness. Those politicians and activist judges who diminish those rights and define a mother's right to choose as more important than those rights of the "created" life are in violation of basic principles in America.

Without the due process for modification of Article V of our Constitution, liberal politicians and activist judges are in violation of the contract between "we the people" and our government. Any changes to the rights of "we the people" as established in the contract between our federal government and "we the people" in the Constitution are violations to the due process of amendment that is established in Article V of that contract. Any compromises to those rights, especially to the First Amendment cannot be tolerated.

Government-sponsored secularism is the government establishment of a religion. Government limitations on religious expression prohibit the free exercise of religion and abridge religious freedom of speech.

The First Amendment to the Constitution of the United States clearly says:

Congress shall make no law respecting an establishment of religion, or prohibiting the free exercise thereof; or abridging the freedom of speech ....

Those who stretch this to mean something other than what it says are doing the work of an evil one who sent them. And those who compromise with them are also helping the evil one.

Chapter 7
Children

Thanksgiving is such a wonderful holiday. George Washington singled out Thanksgiving more than 200 years ago as a national holiday to say thank you for all of our blessings from God.

On Thanksgiving, 2010, several of us gathered at one family home to celebrate. It was happening all across America.

There were about thirty people at our gathering. Sixteen were between the ages of twenty and forty. They were the children of us older folks. Four were between forty and fifty-five. Three were under twenty. They were the children of our children. Seven of us were over fifty-five. Of the total, three were Hispanic, and two were black. One of the younger adults was pregnant. Together, we looked like a cross section of America.

The group of young adults between twenty and forty opened my eyes to a set of values very different from my own. Maybe this was also happening all across America.

Eleven of the sixteen young adults lived in big cities—Washington, DC, New York, and Boston. Four of them were married. Four were "kinda" engaged—living together. Half were men and half were women. None had children and none were pregnant. The only pregnant woman was in her forties and was not married.

This is what they taught me...

More than half of those young adults do not want to ever get married. They see no reason for marriage. They don't know any married people who are happy. And marriage is too confining for their life styles.

Only four of them want to eventually have children (25%). Ten of them (two-thirds) do not want to ever have any children. Only one of the Caucasians wants to have children. None of them understood the impact of a low birth rate today on the economy of the future.

An older woman spoke up and said that the economy is not a reason for having children, even though this poor economy is a result of not having children forty years ago. She added that the economy should not be the reason to have children. All of the young adults agreed and one went so far to say that if the economy is in trouble in the future from a lack of children now, then they could open up the USA to even more immigration to solve it.

When discussing the growth in the number of government employees, "Cousin" stated that it would be okay with him if everyone in the U.S. worked for the government. He just could not understand why having a high percentage of the work force as government employees was unsustainable. A couple of them understood the problem, most had no clue, and half of them agreed with "Cousin." Half of these young adults thought it okay to have everyone in the U.S. work for the government.

Three of these young adults were partially supported by their parents. One stated that she would have to leave the city and move to the suburbs if her parents did not help her. And that would be horrible. She couldn't stand not living in the city. Another said that he would have to change his work to a job that paid more money rather than pursue his art if his parents did not help him. Three others were still living at home. Those three are in their thirties.

All but three of them liked the fact that the government was providing more benefits to them like healthcare insurance. Because of these government benefits, they did not have to worry about those things—like when their parents took care of them. Two owned their own homes, two others previously owned their homes and did not want to ever own one again. All the others either lived with their parents or rented their homes.

Only three of them ever went to church. And that was limited to holidays like Christmas and Easter.

Only a quarter of them—all with college degrees and one a citizen of the UK—understood that Thanksgiving Day is a day of thanksgiving to God for our blessing in America as established by George Washington. Three quarters of them did not understand this and they were all college educated.

All of these young adults came from middle or upper income families.

What have we done in America? How did these young adults get such a different set of values than their parents?

The young adults today were raised by TV, video games, CDs, and the educational system in America. Eighty-five percent of their mothers worked while someone else imparted a moral code to their children.

Liberals have long understood that if they controlled the formulation of the value system of children, then that would insure a larger army for them in the future. And so liberals concentrated on dominating entertainment, media, and education. The results are a generation of young adults with a very liberal value system, a generation of white young adults with a birth rate that will result in negative growth to the white population, and a generation of young adults who expect the government to take care of them.

A blogger on Free Republic wrote the following email to me. I've edited it to highlight the sections about children.

From WorldviewDad (11/26/2010 11:38:54 AM PST):

Interesting discussion on a Thanksgiving... it kinda sounds like the conversation that I had with my in-laws (both in their 80's). They are concerned about the direction that the country is heading and are asking similar questions..."what can be done?"....

In the Scriptures, God has placed the responsibility of raising children and educating them into the hands of the family... as a culture we have placed this into the hands of the government. We, as families, need to take back this responsibility....

.... Let's follow a child from birth to their early 20's... The baby is born and after the six to twelve weeks of FMLA time is placed into day care so that mom can return to work. This is the baby's life for the first several years and then things change when it is four or five years of age... mom and dad are happier now because they no longer have to pay for daycare since baby is now able to go to public school... one less expense.

This continues for several years...

So the child now graduates and looks back at life to realize that he had the "good life", mom and dad both worked so that the family could have the new cars, multiple TVs, multiple computers, multiple video game systems, and he did get his own cell phone at the age of 10 years old... yep, mom and dad are there to provide "stuff" for me... they have learned the lesson well. If life is about ME then why would I want to have children... they will use up the resources that I could use on myself... why would I want to get married... my spouse will want to use up some of my resources... why would I take care of mom and dad when they are older... they will just use up the resources that I want to use on myself... why would I go to church?... they have no answers and just want some of my resources that I want to use on myself. The answer... the government will take care of all of that stuff... it took care of me when I was a child...

...the short answer is to stop feeding the system and educate the people about their God given responsibilities.

Hope I did not ramble on too long... God bless.

Today, one in 600 Americans is a soldier in the military while one in 200 Americans is a lawyer. The USA has three times more lawyers than it has soldiers.

Why? Because our children have been brainwashed into thinking that being a lawyer is better than giving service to the country as a soldier. The problems caused by having such a litigious society are overwhelming, and the problems caused by not having loyalty to the USA as part of the education of our young is destroying America. And we allowed it to happen by what our children are taught in schools.

Jamaica is a very poor country. It has dirt streets with pot holes the size of small meteor craters. Houses made of concrete or tin or cardboard. Many without plumbing—no running water. But, Jamaica has a very high intelligence level. If you have ever been to the residential areas in Kingston, Jamaica, then you have witnessed real poverty. Drugs. Crime. Sexual abuse. Even the most poor in the USA are rich in comparison the general population in Jamaica. So how can such an educated people like the Jamaicans be so poor? So deprived?

In the U.S., we have been led by intellectuals to believe that "information is power." Jamaica has learned the hard way that "what you do with information is power." Therefore, they now preach: "skill is power." That sign, "skill is power," sits on the buildings of St. Patrick's Foundation as it prepares young people to enter the work force. Monsignor Albert has dedicated his life at St. Patrick's Foundation to helping these people "do" more with their knowledge.

Our children have been brainwashed to believing that intelligence for the sake of intelligence is important. They have been deprived of the fact that the pioneers, industrialists, inventors, doctors, and religious people who founded America did something with their knowledge. Their application of knowledge was the reason why the USA became the most admired nation in the world. That application of knowledge is measured in the form of profits and customers and business size. Monsignor Albert understands this. Jamaicans understand this. American intellectuals do not. And intellectuals/teachers are brainwashing our children to be like them.

So what do conservatives do to correct this brainwashing of our children by liberals who are in control of the media, entertainment, and education? WorldViewDad says to stop feeding the system. That is a good start. WorldViewDad points out that the system is government controlled education, liberal controlled entertainment and media, and the stranglehold placed on society and organizations by lawyers.

Stop feeding the system.

Children are the future. Stop feeding them to the government run education system. Stop feeding them to the entertainers. Stop feeding them to the media.

Save. Our heritage needs to be saved. And the first place to save it is in our schools. The next place is in our holidays. On Thanksgiving, do you remember to thank God as done by George Washington when he established the holiday? Or how about discussing with your children why Americans celebrate Independence Day? Or how about reading the Declaration of Independence on the Forth of July to your children? Is Christmas only a time to exchange gifts, or do you discuss with your children the impact of Jesus on the world?

How much time do you spend with your children? Do they feel loved? If so, then maybe they will see the joys of having their own children and the birth rate will increase enough to at least maintain the population without immigration.

The American heritage needs to be saved. And it starts at home.

Challenge. When was the last time that you went to a school board meeting and challenged what it is doing? If you are a parent, or a grandparent, or a local taxpayer—even without children—then you have a vested interest in what is being done by your local school board. It answers to you. The local school system is your employee. Your taxes pay the teachers' salaries. Give it direction and inspect its work just like you would do to an employee.

When was the last time that you challenged your children as to what entertainment they are watching? When was the last time that you turned off the program that your children were watching because it was inappropriate or presented items of which you do not approve? When was the last time that you told your children that those entertainers who poke fun at conservatives are full of crap?

When was the last time that you told your children that you disagreed with them? Especially about the Obamacare "insurance" legislation or about Obama having a proper set of principles or enough executive experience?

Do you require your children to review their homework with you each night? Do you make them work for their spending money, or a portion of their college expenses?

Challenge is the tool of a parent in guiding children. If you are not challenging your children, then who is giving them their guidance?

Talk the Talk. What is your set of values? Do your children hear you discuss them?

My father would take us sons out to practice baseball, football, track, golf, and hockey. He loved to teach us. He loved to watch us grow. He loved to watch us compete with each other and he taught us how to compete with each other and still remain brothers.

What sticks out to me the most about his lessons was one day when we brothers were golfing with my father. He watched me hit a drive into a group of trees. He then looked at me and said: "no one else will know what you do with that ball. No one else will know if you hit it from where it lies or if you move it. But you will know. And you will then know whether you are trustworthy or not."

His comment stuck with me for the last forty-five years.

Do your children know what is important to you?

Evidently, Bill Clinton has a very limited set of values. They are mostly about power and enjoyment—any enjoyment—as long as he doesn't get caught. When Bill got impeached for perjury, did you talk to your children about it? Did they understand that Bill got caught lying under oath? Did they understand that he lied to his family and to the country? Did you explain how it would be hard to ever trust Bill about anything again?

And why didn't you discuss it with them? Was it because the lie was about sex? If so, then your children just learned from you that lies about sex are okay.

Our children are listening to us every day. We need to talk the talk every day. Is God important? Is a strong work ethic important? Is independence important? Is loyalty important? Is America important? And how about the Declaration of Independence and the Constitution of the United States?

My mother would watch TV shows and movies with us three sons. We discussed what we saw. She imparted to us her sense of charity—of helping others. Since my mother's family came to the USA from Syria, she was always conscious of how others viewed her. She was keenly aware of freedom and liberty in America. One time, while we watched the movie *The Ten Commandments* with Charlton Heston, my mother looked at each of us and asked if we understood why Moses led the Jews out of Egypt? Did we understand why her grandparents came to the USA from Syria? She then explained the importance of freedom and self-determination.

My daughter is thirty-two years old and we still have these discussions.

What is important to you? Do your children, your grandchildren, your friends' children, and your nieces and nephews... understand what you think should be important to them?

Good conservatives need to talk the talk. It is part of conserving what is good in America—part of saving America.

Walk the Walk. There are many ways to help children in today's world see conservatives walk the walk.

Most schools send their students on field trips. This is a chance to volunteer to help. One of educators' favorite projects is to have the children volunteer for "Habitat for Humanity." Go with them. And while you work side by side with the children, discuss your views. Let them see that conservatives help others, and then also help them learn conservative principles at the same time.

How about Boy Scouts and Girl Scouts? Get your children to join and join with them. Some of the most joyful times that my daughter shared with me were when she was part of the "Indian Princess" program at the YWCA. We joined as a daughter/father team. We laughed. We worked on projects together. We discussed values. We discussed conservative values.

Do not let the government raise your children. So many American adults send their children to school to be a baby sitter because those parents are so busy with their adult lives. Look in our inner cities where the government has been raising the children for the last forty years. The track record is horrible. Children who are born out of wedlock in the inner cities have grown to 70 percent from 20 percent. With higher numbers of children raised by single parents, scholastic achievement has cratered to an all time low. Crime has increased. Drugs are everywhere. Gangs rule the afternoons. Our children learn more about sex education and alternative life styles than they learn about math and science. Government parenting ruins children as teachers impose their set of values on children without oversight by parents.

Walk the walk and teach your children a set of values to help them live good lives. Do not let the state raise your children. Government parenting is a failure. Good parenting takes a family, not a village—especially not a government-run village.

How much time do you spend with your children? Do you watch them play or do you play with them? Do you go fishing together? Do you go hiking together? Do you play catch together? Do you do homework together? Do you eat dinner with your children at least four nights a week?

Some time ago, so long ago that it is hard for me to remember the source, an article appeared discussing the most common ingredient among those families who have the least problems with their children, who have the happiest families, and who have the lowest percentage of divorce.

That most common ingredient was camping.

Of course it was camping. Camping provides quality time at its best. The parents and children are participants together rather than the parents purely being observers. When you go on a car trip together to go camping, you sing, you play car games, and you discuss life. When you camp, you cook together and do tasks together. Your children experience love from their parents. They learn family values.

Okay, so there are many adults who say that they are not ready for such a commitment to children. They like their adult life, adult friends, adult vacations, and adult careers too much to surrender so much to raising children—so they don't have any children. They are also the ones who tend to justify abortion as a woman's right to choose. They would rather kill the unborn child for convenience than give up their adult life style. But at least they are honest.

So let me say this. In history, those societies that stopped having an adequate amount of children to at least replace the population—like Rome did in 500 A.D.—eventually died.

The Caucasian societies in Europe and the USA will eventually die if they do not increase the birth rate of the intrinsic populations to at least two children per woman.

No children... no future.

Those societies who stop having children lose the essence of staying young. They age as the average age of the society gets older because there are not enough children to keep the average age lower in both a chronological sense and in a psychological sense. That is the most grievous problem facing America and Western Europe today. It affects everything. The economy. Innovation. Energy. The spirit of a nation. The legacy of a people.

A society without enough childbirth is an aging society, and an aging society is a dying society.

Of course, it makes no sense to purely have children to keep chronological balance in a society. People need to have children because they want them, because they love them. At the same time, if a society is voluntarily not having enough children to replace itself, then that should be a warning that the values of that society are decaying. The natural drive for creating life has diminished. The natural drive of a society to survive is dying.

The tolerance towards abortion, gay marriage, and single life styles in America is the result of an attitude of a dying society. Those are the symptoms of a set of values that lead to the death of a nation. The real issue is that America does not cherish life creation as our Founding Fathers did.

Let me say this again from earlier in this book:

A society, a culture, that does not have enough childbirth to replace its self is a dying society, culture. The white people in America and Europe are not having enough children to replace themselves. So the white society, culture, is a dying society.

White America has an attitude problem concerning life creation. And that attitude problem will destroy America. Megan Fox wrote "An Open Letter to Second Wave Feminists: You Failed" on December 2, 2010 for David Horwitz's *News Real* blog. Her letter points out how feminists chose careers rather than children, and how they chose to be single rather than married. She writes: "You chose a plan of action to lead future generations of women, your daughters, down the road of abortion, birth control, and away from traditional family structures. What you failed to anticipate was that every action has a reaction. Man up. It's reaction time." Then she continues later in her letter: "I refuse to credit Second Wave feminism with anything but the destruction of women. From taking them out of the home and jailing them in new prisons (with cubicles) away from their children who are now suffering, to the generations of young women throwing their sexuality away on anything that moves (and who can't figure out why no one respects them)."

She seems to hit the ball squarely in the middle. The modern feminists in Western Societies do not want families. They do not want to follow the traditional values of society. They do not want to raise their own children. And many of them do not want to have children at all.

No children... no future.

So it is up to conservatives to blunt the effects of these modern female liberals, of which many are teaching our children in classrooms. It is up to conservatives to walk the walk and live conservative values by having and raising our own children.

Now let me add that this next item is the last thing that conservatives should do to walk the walk.

And last, we conservatives need to take our children to church. We need to show our children that we walk the walk all the way into church.

Compromise Selfishly. What compromise would you accept that affects the values established in your children? Is it okay to kill? Or steal? Or lie?

There was an expression used many years ago when a young lady lost her virginity outside of marriage. The expression was that "she was compromised." The expression was used to explain that some guy got her to "compromise" her principles. Usually that guy who got her to compromise was some young man who extracted sexual favor from her as repayment for his attention. It was compromise.

Just like that young man, liberals got conservatives to compromise with them so they could eventually screw them.

So let's discuss again what you will accept as compromise to the values that you want your children to have.

Do you want them to learn:

- Personal independence or dependence on government?

- That marriage is between a man and a woman or that alternate lifestyles are also marriage?

- That it is OK to lie?

- That the unborn child is not created by God at conception?

- That redistribution of wealth is not theft?

- That envy, coveting, is an OK method of motivation?

- That careers are more important than motherhood and fatherhood?

- That cheating on taxes, on spouses, and on employers is OK if it is not discovered?

What compromises in values are you willing to allow to be taught to your children and grandchildren?

Chapter 8
Free Enterprise and Private Ownership

The freedoms that our founding fathers articulated included a free flow of goods and capital through an unconstrained free enterprise system. The only exceptions to this by our founding fathers were in order to protect America from monopolies and to establish the U.S. Post Office. Ownership of goods, assets, and property is a cornerstone to freedom. According to InvestorWords.com, the definition of free enterprise is:

> *"Business governed by the laws of supply and demand, not restrained by government interference, regulation or subsidy… called free market."*

And our Constitution of the United States defines the authority of the government towards commerce in Article I, Section 8, "Powers of Congress," that Congress has the power:

> *"To regulate Commerce with foreign Nations, and among the several States, and with the Indian Tribes;"*

Congress has repeatedly used this "commerce clause" in the Constitution to make thousands of laws affecting everything from constructing bridges to mandating that every American must purchase healthcare "insurance"—except government employees and unions and selected states who voted for Obamacare. Every one of those "regulations" violates the free enterprise *laws of supply and demand , not restrained by government interference, regulation or subsidy.*

So, what exactly does the term "regulate" mean? If you are "regulating" the flow of water through a water faucet, then that typically means that a valve is turned to increase or decrease the volume of water to achieve a desired rate of flow. So how does mandating that everyone purchase "insurance" meet any definition of "regulation" without interfering with an individual's right to free enterprise and ownership of personal well being?

Since Obamacare forces everyone to purchase "insurance," it is obvious that the real intention of Obamacare is to regulate—change the rate of flow—of insurance policies to increase the number of customers for insurance companies. So are Americans free? Do we have free markets? Or are Americans really "regulated?"

Jack Tymann is a well-respected executive. He was previously a president at Westinghouse and is currently the chairman of an alternative energy company. Jack made the point that what the founding fathers really gave to America is a free enterprise system. That free enterprise system has allowed for competition, which encouraged the innovations that allowed the USA to be the dominant producer of goods for the last 100 years. Freedom also includes risk, and when corporations or industries or unions are allowed to remove risk by government intervention, then some of the freedom of a free enterprise system is lost. He makes the point that every time that government has stepped into the situation and "regulated" the market, the USA has lost effectiveness and efficiency. The amount of examples includes the Federal Reserve, the SEC, Fannie Mae, Freddie Mac, the Post Office, oil drilling, nuclear power sites, and rail transportation. Every one of those situations became a failure with government "regulation."

The key to free enterprise is personal property rights. As compared to so many failed socialistic countries, the USA thrived because it allowed individual ownership of property and self. That basic principle exploits the basic instinct of selfishness in every person. It is the basic drive to eventually reach enlightened selfishness. The basic rights of "life, liberty, and the pursuit of happiness" were guaranteed to every American at time of "creation" until the liberal dominance of government and courts over the last century replaced it with dominance of the "general welfare" of the masses.

The Congress, with a complicit judicial branch, used the commerce clause and the welfare clause to systematically limit the rights of the individual. The needs of the society became more important than the rights of the individual for all sorts of things like eminent domain and forced purchase of healthcare "insurance." The government allowed unions to control the availability of labor without "regulating" their practices, even though the Constitution clearly calls for regulation or elimination of monopolies. The monopolies of labor established by unions, and sanctioned by government have harmed free enterprise tremendously.

It is my argument that restrictions to free enterprise for the general welfare actually harm the general welfare of Americans. The extreme example is union control of the supply of labor. Because of that control, Americans face higher prices for goods and the loss of manufacturing to foreign nations, which causes a leakage to the USA money supply.

These acts of the USA government are killing the very characteristics of free enterprise and private ownership that created the great successes in America. Government is killing the golden goose with "regulations" and is implementing more "regulations" and more government to correct the very problems that it created.

Jack wrote this in an email to me:

Today, property rights are greatly diminished from the early days. Theft by the government of property in the form of taxes is endemic. Redistribution of wealth is held on a high pedestal, but it is just theft in its most basic form.... Successful economic systems are not particularly dependent on the form of political system.... Take China as an example. It is governed by anything but a democracy yet it has found a way to promote free enterprise inside a dictatorship. The success of China since taking this tact is indeed outstanding...

In the United States, we made the assumption that if we followed the principles of democracy, we would remain great. But democracy has been destroying free enterprise in the process. It revolves around the tyranny of the majority. The majority applies rules and regulations to the minority which are little different than those of a Soviet dictator. Here the minorities are those elements of the population who are trying to make progress; and the politicians are appealing to the majority who benefit from more wealth redistribution. We are close to that magic number where 50% of the population is government dependent. If we don't stop this slide away from free enterprise, we too will be a third world nation.

We've promoted democracy throughout the world when we should have been promoting free enterprise...

We must begin to minimize government, stop redistribution of wealth and promote free enterprise.

Dr. Rick Booth, a contributor on our email exchange wrote the following comments:

> *It just dawned on me. You state that "free enterprise" was the by-product of the Constitution. No, the Declaration of Independence, the Constitution, and our country, were the byproducts of free enterprise.*

Tyranny of the majority. The majority is a mass organization. Liberals used democracy to organize those "Have-Nots" and those "Want-Mores" into a mass organization of people who receive benefits from the government at the expense of those who are the "Haves." That is government-sanctioned theft. It is absolutely contrary to the values documented in our Declaration and our Constitution by our Founding Fathers. It is another example of how our federal government—all three branches—conspires to violate the contract between "we the people" and the federal government without the due process of Article V, the amendment process. Walter E. Williams, professor of Economics at George Mason University wrote this in his article "Moral or Immoral Government" in Townhall.com, Dec 8, 2010:

> *James Madison, the father of our Constitution, stood on the floor of the House to object, saying, "I cannot undertake to lay my finger on that article of the Constitution which granted a right to Congress of expending, on objects of benevolence, the money of their constituents." Did James Madison miss something in the Constitution?*

You might answer, "He forgot the general welfare clause." No, he had that covered, saying, "If Congress can do whatever in their discretion can be done by money, and will promote the General Welfare, the Government is no longer a limited one, possessing enumerated powers, but an indefinite one."

If we accept the value of self-ownership, it is clear that most of what Congress does is clearly immoral. If this is bothersome, there are two ways around my argument. The first is to deny the implications of self-ownership. The second is to ask, as Speaker Nancy Pelosi did when asked about the constitutionality of Obamacare, "Are you serious? Are you serious?"

Immorality in government lies at the heart of our nation's problems. Deficits, debt and runaway government are merely symptoms. What's moral and immoral conduct can be complicated, but needlessly so. I keep things simple and you tell me where I go wrong.

My initial assumption is that we each own ourselves. I am my private property and you are yours. If we accept the notion that people own themselves, then it's easy to discover what forms of conduct are moral and immoral. Immoral acts are those that violate self-ownership. Murder, rape, assault and slavery are immoral because those acts violate private property. So is theft, broadly defined as taking the rightful property of one person and giving it to another.

The list of those violations by our federal government to ownership of self and private property, by the legislative branch, the executive branch, and the judicial branch, is long.

Federal and local governments have been decreasing the rights of individuals through the tax system and through regulations like Obamacare. These are just a few:

- Progressive income tax

- Estate tax

- Cumulative tax throughout the manufacturing supply chain

- GM bail out

- Financial bail out

- Benefit system

- Obamacare

- Exemption of Obamacare for government workers and union employees

Every one of them decreased the rights of individuals to accumulate wealth and to control their own lives. These actions decreased competition between factions of labor and decreased competition between providers of goods in a free enterprise nation. They harm the "general welfare" of a nation.

Along with the right to ownership comes the responsibility of risk. Government used the excuse of "general welfare" to eliminate the risk of ownership for those that the government wanted to protect from risk. The government bailed out pension funds of unions under the justification of helping the general welfare of Americans. It imposed mandatory healthcare "insurance" under the same justification. The long list includes: banks, Fannie Mae, Freddie Mac, GM, SEIU, and NEA who all benefited from actions in a free marketplace and then did not have to suffer the risk of those actions. In the process, the government killed a little more of the freedom of ownership with each action that eliminated risk.

So what do conservatives do to save free enterprise and private ownership from death by a liberal controlled government?

Save. Life, liberty, and the pursuit of happiness are at stake.

Once a government can define what liberties are allowed and which ones are not, then liberty is dead. Once a government can define what happiness means to the individual, then the freedom to pursue individual happiness is dead. This liberal dominated government is killing private ownership and free enterprise. It is saying that free enterprise and private ownership cannot be part of the definition of what is important in an individual's life. It is saying that free enterprise and private ownership is not included in liberty. It is saying that free enterprise and private ownership are not part of an individual's pursuit of happiness.

The whole concept of "it takes a village" is in total opposition to individualism. The whole concept of a communal society is destructive to individual rights of private ownership of property and self-determination.

So when a government takes from one to give to another, it has eliminated the ability of the individual to own the use of the capital. When the government spends taxes on what that government thinks is important—like bailouts or redistribution of wealth or contributions to nonprofit organizations that it prefers or to foreign governments—then the rights of the individual are violated. When the government forces an individual to purchase something that the individual does not want like healthcare "insurance," then the individual has lost control of the use of individually owned capital.

Free enterprise and private ownership are part of the basic principles of freedom in America. Once the government can stipulate what can be owned and what cannot, then it can stipulate anything that it wants to stipulate. Once the government can order what must be purchased for healthcare, then it can stipulate how else you must spend your capital. Once the government can dictate what an individual can do with his/her own life, then all freedom is at risk.

We need to save the ability for free enterprise and the ability to own our own lives and our own property in order to save freedom and liberty.

Challenge. Do you have the right to not purchase something? You might say, "yes" if you don't think about it too much.

The local government takes payment from you for the public school system in the form of property taxes and other local taxes. Those funds are used to pay teachers who probably belong to unions. Those union members make payments to their unions who use a portion of it to get liberal politicians elected.

Without your permission, you are paying for:

- Teachers who you might not want.

- Unions that continue to get politicians elected that you might not want.

- Subjects taught that you might not want taught.

How many other purchases are made on your behalf that you might not want? How much money is spent for purchases that you did not authorize? Healthcare and college educations for illegal immigrants. Bribes to foreign leaders. Twenty-five percent of the costs of the United Nations. Subsidies to farms and ethanol production.

The list of things that the government purchases for tax payers without permission is quite long. In the winter of 2010, Congress tried to get legislation passed that included more than 6,000 earmarks without permission of the electorate, or even a review by our representatives.

The leak of thousands of documents by WikiLeaks exposed how the government spends the money of the tax payers for so many things that are not authorized by taxpayers like the espionage performed by the State Department under instructions by Hillary Clinton. Yes, this is the same Hillary Clinton who illegally had 900 FBI files about individuals in her possession when Bill was president. How does she use this information? Does she blackmail people?

WikiLeaks also exposed how government agencies of union employees issued orders that contracts to the private sector could only be issued to companies who employed union workers.

But what did the media concentrate on reporting to America? The liberal media/entertainment cartel concentrated its reporting on the leak and not on the content, when the content of what this government is doing was certainly more important than the leak. Don't the clandestine actions of the Clinton State Department seem important to you? Don't the usurping actions of the Obama administration seem important to you? The media once again distracted America from what was important.

Government agencies spend tax money from citizens. Are they spending it how you want it spent? Are they spending it on what you want?

These government actions erode free enterprise and individual property ownership as the government takes more and more ownership of the capital of the private sector for spending on its priorities.

How can the USA claim to have "Business governed by the laws of *supply and demand, not restrained by* government interference, regulation or subsidy... free enterprise" if we are forced to purchase labor from a single source like unions or if we must pay for public education without any competition for education funds?

The only way to stop this erosion of property rights and of free enterprise is to challenge every action of the government.

So how do we challenge the government? By vocally questioning everything. Call your congressman and senators about every item that you find to be abhorrent. Call your state representatives and question everything done by local government officials. Attend town hall meetings and expose all of the government infringements in front of others so all citizens learn how property rights and free enterprise are being killed.

Slow down the actions of governments. Cause gridlock until the actions of government are understood. Look at the Obamacare legislation. It was 3000 pages. Congress and the public were given three days to read it and understand it, and question it before the vote was taken. Practically every Democrat voted for it. It is hard to believe that any of them read it before voting for it. And when questioned about it, Nancy Pelosi remarked, "We have to pass it in order to see what is in it."

That is wrong! How could those Democrats know if there was something wrong in the legislation with only three days to read 3000 pages? Those Democrats voted politically rather than in the best interests of America.

As long as politicians think that you don't care, then they will continue their encroachment of ownership of private property, especially capital, and of free enterprise.

"We the people" must challenge governments about every dollar that they spend. The government works for the citizens. The government employees, including judges and teachers, are employees of "we the people." Just as any employer would ask for an accounting of time and results, "we the people" must demand an accounting of time and results from government agencies.

Oh, government employees will state that they provide reports and information to our elected representatives and judges—but those reports are actually being sent to staffers. Those staffers, those judges, and those representatives are also government employees. "We the people" should challenge them, all of them, on every occasion.

Talk the Talk. Do you believe in free enterprise? Do you believe in private ownership of property? Do you think that governments are abusing free enterprise and private ownership? Then speak up! Do your neighbors know how you feel about this? Do those people know where you work? The bad guys are wearing white hats about this. They are talking loudly about how the work done by government is helping the less privileged and how the rights of individual property ownership and free enterprise need to be regulated for the benefit of the masses. They have the microphone. So speak up! Take the microphone away from them and speak up! Free enterprise and property ownership are part of "life, liberty, and the pursuit of happiness." Capital is property. Any infringement on how you use your capital is an infringement on free enterprise and property ownership. Talk about it.

Walk the Walk. When it comes to demonstrating your belief in free enterprise and property ownership, walking the walk is easy—use your purchasing power.

Do not ever buy a GM car. GM had an opportunity to break the back of unions who are pricing manufacturing out of the USA. GM could have declared bankruptcy and restructured its contracts with unions. Instead, GM took a bail out of money that made the U.S. government the major stockholder, owner, of GM. Unions were kept whole while the stockholders and bondholders of GM suffered. GM executives and the government conspired to help unions at the expense of stockholders and bondholders. GM executives and government sided against free enterprise and capital ownership.

GM was a coward. GM sold out free enterprise. GM capitulated to the very unions that caused its financial problems. GM sold out an opportunity to reduce the impact of the increasing costs of unions that are making American products uncompetitive.

Do not ever buy another GM product. Do not ever buy any product from any company who does what GM did. Walk the walk.

There are many other ways to walk the walk. Vote "no" on those bond requests of your local governments. Force them to live within their budgets. Vote "no" on pay increases for government employees. Make employment in the private sector look better than government employment, and vote "no" on any tax increases of any kind.

Governments continue to tell us that they need more money because of increases in demand for their services. OK, then cut back on other services. When governments tell us that costs are increasing because of more people, then we should absolutely vote "no" because an increase to people should automatically be providing governments more revenue without having to increase taxes.

Walk the Walk. Stop purchasing goods from companies who support more government. GE is one of those companies. GE receives lots of contracts from government agencies. And the CEO of GE has been one of the most frequent visitors to the Obama White House. GE owned NBC and its affiliates. So naturally GE used its media abilities to subtly promote the government agenda. Stop purchasing goods from GE.

Push for school vouchers. Your children get a better education with more education competition and, with fewer students in public education, fewer teachers will be needed and fewer dollars will flow into the NEA teachers union.

Today, the U.S. Post Office is the prime example of how government and liberals think. Because of competition to the postal service from delivery companies, FAX machines, couriers, and the Internet, demand for post offices products is falling as it becomes less and less competitive. The response by the post office to more competition has been to increase the price of mail. The price to consumers for postal stamps has increased more than three times faster than inflation. That is the reaction of liberals, of government. They raise prices rather than figure out how to compete and cut costs.

Federal Express is one of those competitors to the post office. Fred Smith started Federal Express in the 1970s after he noticed a need for overnight deliveries. He wrote a paper in college about his idea on how to provide overnight delivery service and his professor graded it as a C-. Since then, competition from Federal Express revolutionized delivery service throughout the world. That is free enterprise. It is private ownership of corporate assets to provide what the market place wanted "by the laws of supply and demand, not restrained by government interference, regulation or subsidy."

If Fred Smith's idea had been left to educators or the federal government's post office, it would never have happened.

Walk the Walk. Ways to defeat those who are destroying capitalism, free enterprise, private ownership, are all around you. Use your purchasing power and walk the walk. Use your voting power and get rid of the politicians who interfere with the free market.

Compromise Selfishly. What is the middle ground about free enterprise and ownership of self/private property that can be compromised without diminishing free enterprise and private ownership? Yes, there are some things that need to be done by government. Certainly, air traffic control needs to be a function of government. If there are 10,000 commercial flights in the USA every day, then some type of coordination is needed to provide security to the travelers. Those air traffic controllers went on strike when Ronald Reagan was president. The air traffic control union wanted more for its labor. This put the entire air travel industry in jeopardy. The air traffic controllers thought that their monopoly of labor had the airline industry at their command. Ronald Reagan recognized a monopoly when he saw it. Unions are a monopoly of labor. So he treated the union as a monopoly and fired all the traffic controllers. He then hired some of them back and hired new ones from outside of the union. He caused competition and used free enterprise to provide a lower cost with more service to America. So what was the compromise? Traffic controllers are government employees. But they were also treated as a monopoly. Yes. There is middle ground. Yes, there is compromise as long as that compromise allows for free enterprise in the process and recognizes unions and government employees for what they are (including public school teachers)—monopolies and servants to the public.

The government continues to enact laws and taxes that apply to most people, but also excludes some. The primary example is Obamacare where unions, several states, and government employees are exempt from it. To date, more than a thousand exemptions to Obamacare have been granted, mostly to Democrat/Obama supporters. Bernard George sent me an email with this suggested amendment to our Constitution. His Twenty-eighth Amendment would be an acceptable compromise to the current Sixteenth Amendment:

Proposed 28th Amendment to the United States Constitution:

"Congress shall make no law or tax that applies to the citizens of the United States that does not apply equally to ALL OF the Senators and/or Representatives and/or all federal employees; and, Congress shall make no law or tax that applies to the Senators and/or Representatives and/or all federal employees that does not apply equally to ALL OF the LEGAL citizens of the United States of America."

All current laws *must* adjust to this new mandate!

Chapter 9
Taxes

Taxes provide the government with revenue to pay for its work. Unlike with free enterprise, there is no method of equating supply with demand to price the services provided by government. So as revenues from taxes increase or decrease, the government either grows or shrinks.

The Tea Parties (TEA = Taxed Enough Already) are determined to drive down taxes and tax revenues to ultimately drive down the size of government.

At the same time, government employees (unions, SEIU and NEA) are driven to drive up taxes so there is more money to pay government employees, including teachers. The teachers' strike in Wisconsin in February 2011 was a great example of this. To fix the state's financial problem, the voters elected a Republican legislature to reduce government costs. When the legislature proposed reducing the teacher work force by 5,000 teachers or cutting the amount of benefits provided to teachers, the teachers went on strike. So then the legislature proposed eliminating collective bargaining with "right to work" laws that are used in so many states who do not have financial problems. In reaction, the teachers violated their contract and went on strike in even more deliberate violation of their contract with full support from Barack Hussein Obama and the Democratic Party.

The unions have been effective. As stated earlier in this book, government workers outnumber the combined workers in construction and manufacturing in the USA after being less than half the number of workers in construction and manufacturing only forty years ago, and government workers are paid substantially more than their counterparts in private industry. As shown in *Save America Now,* the average worker in America now pays 54 percent of income to the combined taxes of federal and local governments to pay for government workers/programs.

While the media and the government have Americans focused on income taxes, governments manipulate many other taxes to continue to increase government revenues. The *Wall Street Journal* of December 24, 2010 stated: "Cities across the nation are raising property taxes, largely citing rising pension and healthcare costs for their employees." Those increased property taxes will affect everyone. Even rents will increase because of those increased property taxes.

Rather than decreasing the costs of operation, the government increases taxes to pay for government employees while the private sector must cut expenses to survive. Without competition, the government can charge whatever it wants for its services. Without allowing individuals to pay for only the portions of government that they want, the government is allowed to operate without the constraints of a free market.

The government determines what it wants to do without being accountable to customers. The government charges what wants to charge without any market constraints, and the government can force consumption of its products/programs like it does with Social Security and Obamacare.

Barry Goldwater warned of this creeping government growth in 1960 in his book, *Conscience of a Conservative*. He cautioned that the federal government was expanding too fast because it was growing from a budget of $100 billion per year to $300 billion.

The 2010 federal government spent close to three and a half trillion dollars. That is almost twelve times growth from the government that Goldwater warned us. The federal government grew twelve times in the last fifty years while GDP only grew six times. The size of the federal government is growing at a rate that is two times the growth of the economy. Therefore, federal tax revenues have grown two times faster than the economy. And local taxes have grown even faster.

During that same time, military spending shrunk from fifty percent of the federal budget to twenty percent. While the total federal government grew twelve times, the military grew less than four times. Growth in military spending has been less than the rate of growth to the economy. That actually hurt the economy since the military spends on manufactured products that have a much greater multiplier effect on the economy than does the rest of government spending.

Ninety percent (90%) of the growth to federal government spending in the last fifty years is for non-military reasons.

If this continues, it will break America.

Article I. Section 8—Powers of Congress

The Congress shall have Power To lay and collect Taxes, Duties, Imposts and Excises, to pay the Debts and provide for the common Defense and general Welfare of the United

States; but all Duties, Imposts and Excises shall be uniform throughout the United States;

Amendment 16: Status of Income Tax Clarified.
Ratified February 3, 1913

The Congress shall have power to lay and collect taxes on incomes, from whatever source derived, without apportionment among the several States, and without regard to any census or enumeration.

Where the original intent of taxation was to pay the debts and provide for the common defense and general welfare of the United States, the Sixteenth Amendment to the Constitution allows the federal government to tax income for just about anything that it wants —and in any way that it wants.

Today, tax revenues are used by the federal government to prop up foreign governments, to make payoffs to foreign leaders, to provide money to political operatives like ACORN, to prop up public radio and public television, to subsidize selected industries, to subsidize products without an economic base in the free enterprise system—like ethanol and solar panels—and for thousands of earmarks every year to selected projects like the Alaskan "Bridge to Nowhere." And all of this is justified as providing for the common Defense and general Welfare of the United States.

This is wrong. While the Sixteenth Amendment was meant to give more flexibility for taxation to our elected officials, the Sixteenth Amendment has been abused by politicians to tax America much more than could ever have been imagined and for uses that clearly are not for the common defense and general welfare of the United States.

Again, the Congress and the executive branches have violated the Constitution and the federal judges have allowed them to do it.

As Dick Morris and Eileen McGann pointed out in *The New York Post* on December 23, 2010:

> *High taxes kill states. There can be no better evidence than the 2010 Census. The states that lost House seats because they're shrinking, relative to the nation, had taxes 27 percent higher than the ones that gained seats.*

Of the seven states that don't have a personal income tax, four (Texas, Florida, Nevada and Washington) account for 8 of the 12 seats apportioned to the fastest-growing states.... The trend is unmistakable: The "losing" states drove out their high-income citizens (and middle-income jobs) with heavier tax burdens.

Two of my closest friends do exactly what Dick Morris and Eileen McGann claim. Both Jim and Jack maintain homes, in Maryland and in Florida. Both of them make sure to not be in Maryland more than 179 days per year so they do not have to pay Maryland taxes. And both of them claim permanent residence in Florida where they pay no income taxes. Liberals will claim that taxes do not motivate or de-motivate anyone to live anywhere, but the facts point out something very different. While liberals may not understand how a profit motive drives actions, conservatives do.

So how long will it be until Americans live in other countries to avoid taxes in the USA?

They are already doing it. There are ex-patriots in countries all over the world who moved to escape U.S. taxes. And those companies who place their manufacturing plants outside of the USA or their headquarters outside of the USA to avoid taxes are direct examples of how taxes cause the relocation of people, the outsourcing of manufacturing, and the loss of the producers in society just like Dick Morris and Eileen McGann discovered.

During the 2008 election cycle, the process exposed how those high tax folks like Hillary and Bill Clinton, keep money/ investments outside of the USA. The elite like George Soros and Ted Turner and Oprah Winfrey and Warren Buffet place money outside of the USA to reduce their taxes while they support more socialism for everyone else.

Save. How do we save America? How do we keep the federal government from driving out the producers in society? How do we keep government from killing more jobs in the private sector? One of the keys to saving America is stopping the unlimited ability of government to tax and spend as it wants. We need to replace the Sixteenth Amendment and define defense and general welfare with a tax amendment that limits the government taxing powers and spending powers to those items that are meant for operation of the government and those items explicitly enumerated in the Constitution. And any other spending and/or taxing can only be done by referendum of the electorate.

Challenge. Nancy Pelosi made a comment that when government spends on unemployment it helps put money in the hands of people who buy things, and that helps the economy. She proposed taxing those who work even more to provide more unemployment benefits to the unemployed. By her logic, then we should "unemploy" many more people and put them on unemployment benefits to help the economy.

There are many jobs that people do not take simply because they want other jobs, or want more pay than what is offered.

What is the impending event that would cause an unemployed person to take an undesired job if the government is willing to pay the person to stay unemployed? Where is the magic of free market demand and supply?

Our company, any company, would employ more people if those people could be obtained at lower prices. When the government artificially props up prices with unemployment payments or other subsidies, it negates the process of decreasing prices until total supply is consumed. This is the same problem with farm subsidies and using corn for ethanol. Government interference with a free market hurts all Americans. If Nancy Pelosi's logic were applied in the early 1900s, the USA would still have many out-of-work buggy whip makers.

Nancy Pelosi showed her disdain for the free market system with her remarks and logic. What is worse is that so many Americans accepted her logic without challenging her. Unions hurt the economy and the unemployed by forcing the prices for labor to stay frozen without the ability to drop. And the government is complicit by allowing unions to have monopolies of labor. It is time to challenge all those politicians, those neighbors, those family members who think that it is OK for the government to indefinitely support the unemployed with taxes from American workers. It is time to challenge all those who think that it is OK for governments to tax as they want to pay for anything that they want.

Daniel Mitchell, Ph.D. wrote "The Historical Lessons of Lower Tax Rates" in August of 2003. It was a web memo from The Historical Lessons of Lower Tax Rates *originally published July 19, 1996:*

There is a distinct pattern throughout American history: When tax rates are reduced, the economy's growth rate improves and living standards increase. Good tax policy has a number of interesting side effects. For instance, history tells us that tax revenues grow and "rich" taxpayers pay more tax when marginal tax rates are slashed. This means lower income citizens bear a lower share of the tax burden—a consequence that should lead class-warfare politicians to support lower tax rates.

Conversely, periods of higher tax rates are associated with sub par economic performance and stagnant tax revenues. In other words, when politicians attempt to "soak the rich," the rest of us take a bath. Examining the three major United States episodes of tax rate reductions can prove useful lessons.

The tax cuts of the 1920s

Tax rates were slashed dramatically during the 1920s, dropping from over 70 percent to less than 25 percent. What happened? Personal income tax revenues increased substantially during the 1920s, despite the reduction in rates. Revenues rose from $719 million in 1921 to $1164 million in 1928, an increase of more than 61 percent.

According to then-Treasury Secretary Andrew Mellon:

The history of taxation shows that taxes which are inherently excessive are not paid. The high rates inevitably put pressure upon the taxpayer to withdraw his capital from productive business and invest it in tax-exempt securities or to find other lawful methods of avoiding the realization of taxable income. The result is that the sources of taxation are drying up; wealth is failing to carry its share of the tax burden; and capital is being diverted into channels which yield neither revenue to the Government nor profit to the people.

The Kennedy tax cuts

President Hoover dramatically increased tax rates in the 1930s and President Roosevelt compounded the damage by pushing marginal tax rates to more than 90 percent. Recognizing that high tax rates were hindering the economy, President Kennedy proposed across-the-board tax rate reductions that reduced the top tax rate from more than 90 percent down to 70 percent. What happened? Tax revenues climbed from $94 billion in 1961 to $153 billion in 1968, an increase of 62 percent (33 percent after adjusting for inflation).

According to President John F. Kennedy:

Our true choice is not between tax reduction, on the one hand, and the avoidance of large Federal deficits on the other. It is increasingly clear that no matter what party is in power, so long as our national security needs keep rising, an economy hampered by restrictive tax rates will never produce enough revenue to balance our budget just as it will never produce enough jobs or enough profits... In short, it is a paradoxical truth that tax rates are too high today and tax revenues are too low and the soundest way to raise the revenues in the long run is to cut the rates now.

The Reagan tax cuts

Thanks to "bracket creep," the inflation of the 1970s pushed millions of taxpayers into higher tax brackets even though their inflation-adjusted incomes were not rising. To help offset this tax increase and also to improve incentives to work, save, and invest, President Reagan proposed sweeping tax rate reductions during the 1980s. What happened? Total tax revenues climbed by 99.4 percent during the 1980s, and the results are even more impressive when looking at what happened to personal income tax revenues. Once the economy received an unambiguous tax cut in January 1983, income tax revenues climbed dramatically, increasing by more than 54 percent by 1989 (28 percent after adjusting for inflation).

According to then-U.S. Representative Jack Kemp (R-NY), one of the chief architects of the Reagan tax cuts:

At some point, additional taxes so discourage the activity being taxed, such as working or investing, that they yield less revenue rather than more. There are, after all, two rates that yield the same amount of revenue: high tax rates on low production, or low rates on high production. The rich pay more when incentives to hide income are reduced...

Harmful Spending & Complexity

Lower tax rates are important, but they are not the only critical issue. Both the level of government spending and where that money goes are very important. And even when looking only at tax policy, tax rates are just one piece of the puzzle. If certain types of income are subject to multiple layers of tax, as occurs in the current system, that problem cannot be solved by low rates. Similarly, a tax system with needless levels of complexity will impose heavy costs on the productive sector of the economy.

The facts show that unconstrained taxation by the government is one of the contributors to economic problems. Governments take money from the product producing part of the economy and redirect it to the nonproductive service actions of government. That is a losing strategy. We citizens of America need to challenge this tax and spend attitude of government. We need to question everything that governments do with our money and how they plan to generate revenues to pay for their programs. We need to demand that governments cut current program spending to implement new programs.

The Democratic Congress of 2007-2010 passed a law that required it to include in any legislation how it plans to pay for the program that it authorizes. Jim Bunning, Republican U.S. Senator from Kentucky, challenged legislation in the spring of 2010 to extend unemployment benefits because the legislation lacked how it was to be financed. Jim Bunning had a colorful history. He was a true competitor. He was a major league pitcher who pitched no-hitters in both the American league and the National League. He was part of the Detroit Tigers team who won the World Series. Jim Bunning was accustomed to conflict and stress. So he was ready for the assault from the liberals.

Congress was in violation of its own law by not stating how it planned to pay for the extension by either cutting other programs or stipulating the source for the funds to extend unemployment.

America sat silent. The media missed the point. Just as Saul Alinsky instructed, liberals demonized Bunning as being heartless for obstructing legislation to help the unemployed. It was the same class warfare rhetoric as detailed in *Rules for Radicals*. Even Bunning's own party ignored his pleads. Bunning stood alone in his challenge of Congress. Then, in the fall of 2010, the Tea Party remembered Bunning. He was not running for reelection. The voters threw out the liberal candidate for his senate seat who cast disparagement at Bunning. Rand Paul was elected to replace Bunning and he is even more against government spending than Bunning. The first proposal to the new Senate of 2011 by Paul was to cut government spending for the remainder of 2011 by $500 Billion (close to 15%).

Go Rand! Cut more! Did the rest of the Republicans get the message? Politicians must state how they plan to fund their programs. "We the people" must challenge them to make sure that they do. And when they deliberately mislead America about the costs and/or the funding, like Obama, Pelosi and Reid did about Obamacare, then we must fire them and we must reject their programs.

Jim Bunning was right. We need more Jim Bunnings who will challenge taxing and spending by governments. "We the people" need to challenge government taxing, and spending. When the challenges are made, we conservatives need to give the challengers our full support. And we cannot let the "Alinskies" demonize the challengers.

Talk the talk. NBC and MSNBC carried polls in 2010 that showed most Americans do not want to cut any of the services that are currently provided by governments. The poll also showed that most Americans want taxes to decrease. And the poll went on to state that only 13% of Americans were satisfied with the job being done by the Democratically controlled U.S. Congress. From that, the commentators claimed, "America wants its cake and eat it too. You can't cut taxes and maintain the same level of services." As usual, the liberal media/entertainment cartel was spinning the data. They could not think outside of the liberal box because they are part of the liberal box.

Those polls were simply stating that most Americans think that government spending can be reduced without a loss to the services provided by government. If salaries for government workers are reduced to be in line with the private sector, then the combined federal and local governments can cut a trillion dollars from their costs. What the polls showed was that most Americans think that government is inefficient. And most Americans think that the Democratically controlled Congress of 2010 was a failure at providing services while controlling costs.

Before Obamacare legislation was passed, Rasmussen and Gallup polls showed that two-thirds of America wanted to either scrap Obamacare and start over or wanted to modify it greatly. The polls showed that the number one objective for Americans was to decrease the cost of healthcare without decreasing the quality of healthcare. From that, the media stated that less than half of America wanted to get rid of Obamacare. And that most of America wanted healthcare reform.

The media twisted the data to fit the agenda of the Obama administration.

So what did America get? The liberals relabeled "healthcare reform" to be healthcare "insurance" and America got healthcare "insurance" mandated for everyone that increased healthcare insurance prices and decreased healthcare benefits.

During the debates about Obamacare, the OMB issued a report that stated that Obamacare would decrease the deficit in a ten year time period. Liberals used that information to justify their votes for Obamacare. A couple of months later, the OMB issued another report changing their original estimate with a statement that Obamacare would increase the deficit in that same ten year time period. The only way to make Obamacare "deficit neutral" would be to increase taxes associated with it. A year later, the OMB now states that Obamacare has $1 trillion of additional taxes in it. Costs to Americans will also increase another $1.4 trillion dollars. In total, that is $2.4 trillion in additional costs to Americans.

So the liberal run Congress voted to make Obamacare the law of the land, even though it would increase the deficit and even though two-thirds of America opposed it. In *The American*, a journal of the American Enterprise Institute, on December 26, 2010 Mark J. Perry and Robert Dell state:

> *The Patient Protection and Affordable Care Act ("ObamaCare") ignores the government's role in creating a crisis of runaway health costs and a low health-outcome-to-cost ratio... Many of the "Tea Party" Republicans swept into power in the November midterm elections ran on a platform of replacing or reforming ObamaCare. Their success at the polls partially reflects the correct perception of the majority of informed Americans that persistent problems in U.S. healthcare stem primarily from government failure.*

When the government spends money, it costs the taxpayers more than when it is done by private enterprise. Period. And the government never implements any programs that do not cost more and provide less than it anticipates.

Why?

1. Because the government is a monopoly that is outside of the laws of a free market—free enterprise. The government has no competition. It is run by union-oriented bureaucrats. Therefore, it is not efficient and is not effective.

2. Because the government is subject to influences from its donors. Legislators pay back debts to their supporters by passing legislation and spending money that benefits their donors at the expense to the rest of America. In this case, the donors were the insurance companies and unions. So unions are exempt from Obamacare and insurance companies gain lots of new customers at higher rates while providing less coverage.

So now it is time to talk the talk. Whenever a new program is proposed, that is the time to ask governments, "What is the source for the money for the program?" And if the answer is an increase to taxes—any taxes including fees buried in products like gasoline or added sales taxes like a VAT (value added tax)—then speak up against it.

Any time a program is suggested that increases taxes to pay for it, it is time to speak up and say "no!" Talk the talk.

Ask the simple question, "Where are you going to get the money for the program that you propose?" And then ask, "If the program is so good, then why not let the free market do it?"

As a side note, many liberals believe in Darwinism to explain the evolution of man, survival of the fittest, yet they won't let the free market sort out what ideas should live and which ones should die. They are hypocrites.

In a television interview, Ramsey Clarke stated that the government needed to appropriate $50 billion dollars of seed money to help the ethanol business. He continued saying that the $50 billion was needed to help the ethanol business "start up" even though the ethanol business has been in startup mode for several years. The government sunk several billions of dollars into the ethanol business but Ramsey thinks that more money can come from placing more taxes on gasoline. He neglected the fact that as corn is used to create fuel, the cost of food increases. This is all about demand and supply. The use of corn for ethanol alters the supply of corn to the demand in the food industry, so the price of corn increases. And he neglected the fact that it costs more to make ethanol than to make oil based gasoline because of the competition from the food business and from intrinsic production costs. If the ethanol business is so viable, then why don't private investors come up with the seed money like they have done for so many other ideas like CISCO, FedEx, the auto industry in the 1920s, Apple Computer, cell phones, etc? If farmers are so eager to be in the ethanol business, then why don't they come up with the investment money?

Politicians are wasteful and they pander to their political bases. Waste and pandering are the sure ingredients for continual growth to government and taxes. Ramsey Clarke was showing one more example of how the government is against the free market system and uses taxes to prop up ideas that might not succeed in a free society that practices free enterprise.

Speak up and say, "We are Taxed Enough Already." Talk the talk.

Walk the walk. Do you live within your own means? Do you borrow for items other than your home or your automobiles? It is OK to borrow money to purchase long-term durable goods like mortgages to buy houses and loans to buy cars because the asset is the collateral for the loan and because purchases of durable goods help the economy. There is no sane reason to borrow for non-durable purchases. That includes borrowing money for children's educations. If more children worked to pay for their educations, then less tuition could be afforded and the price for education would drop. Credit cards should only be used as a monetary exchange tool. They should be paid immediately without incurring any interest charges.

If you obtain a mortgage or a home equity loan to obtain money for purchases on the stock market, then you deserve everything and anything that happens to you. With less use of credit for non-durable goods and services, the prices for those goods and services will decrease, including the price for education.

And once you do these things for yourself, then you can demand them of the government.

Compromise selfishly. As stated earlier in this book, the Constitution was written to limit the authority of the federal government. In every case where the limitations have been relaxed (compromised), the government has found ways to abuse that compromise. The Sixteenth Amendment is one of those compromises. It was meant to provide flexibility in raising revenue to fund government operations and instead has been used to increase taxes and spending to levels that were never imagined when the Sixteenth Amendment was written.

Barack Hussein Obama claimed that he was compromising with Republicans when he agreed to extend the Bush tax cuts.

Let me note that the media and liberals disparaged Bush for years because of the tax cuts of 2001. Those tax cuts helped give America one of the most robust economies in history with an unemployment rate about the same as under Bill Clinton at 4.5 percent. In fact, it was a Democratically controlled Senate who approved those tax cuts. Obama reversed his stand about the Bush tax cuts when he made the case in December 2010 about how those tax cuts needed to be extended to help the economy.

Democratic Senator Max Baucus (D-MT) had this to say after the June 8, 2001 signing ceremony for the Bush tax cuts at the White House: "Every day it looks like a better and better decision. In many respects, I think politically I helped the party."

Obama ran against those tax cuts as evil done by Bush to help his wealthy friends. Then he reversed his position in 2010. So is there an apology going to be given to Bush from the media, Democrats, and Obama for their demonizing of Bush? Of course not. Did the Republicans demand an apology? Of course not.

Instead, the Republicans compromised with Obama and allowed him to imbed more benefits to the unemployed as part of extending the tax cuts without stipulating what funds would be used to pay for those benefits even though the law requires that Congress do so. And the tax cuts are temporary instead of permanent. The Republicans compromised again when they did not have to do it. They gave up more conservative principles and their conservative position.

Roanna Brown of California wrote this in an email on December 8, 2010:

Too bad that the current Republicans don't know how to act like winners!!! They HAD the upper hand and they squandered their OPPORTUNITY!!!! Obama knew that if he waited to DEAL with the incoming Republicans he would have had to have given far more than what he gave!!! The new Republicans would not have tolerated an extension of unemployment nor a TEMPORARY EXTENSION of the Bush tax cuts!!!!!!!!!!!!

Roanna Brown sounds like many Tea Party people. If the Republicans continue compromising away the conservative positions, then they will lose the support of those whom they are supposed to represent. They need to compromise selfishly if they wish to represent conservatives.

If there is a compromise, then this is what conservatives should require:

- The tax system should eliminate the progressive increases to tax rates. The rate should be the same for all Americans so the use of class warfare is reduced in politics.

- Deductions should be available equally to everyone. Again, this will also reduce the use of class warfare in politics while helping those who are less fortunate.

- The tax system should be used to incent the population to do things that help improve the general welfare of Americans. For example: if it would help the "general welfare" for Americans if everyone had healthcare insurance, or if it helps the economy if people own homes, or if it helps our national interests if Americans are educated; then the tax system should be used to incent Americans to do those things rather than using penalties to force compliance.

- The system should stop the penalties that could affect married couples or single people. The tax system should be neutral on filing married or filing individually.

- Changes to the income tax rates and deductions should affect all Americans in a way that they are readily visible so that politicians are made accountable for their actions in taxing Americans.

The following tax worksheet incorporates these five policies. The overall principle is that all Americans are treated equally while providing help to those who are less fortunate. These types of changes to our tax system will make it simpler to implement, will stop the political abuses of class warfare, and will stop tax evasion.

This principle of equality must be emphasized by conservatives as the underlying principle for tax policies.

The work sheet on the next page includes two examples (#2 and # 5) of many that were run to determine the amount of income taxes paid in several different scenarios. With this approach, the very wealthy will still pay more than two-thirds of taxes collected by income taxes while those who have less than $50,000 income will probably pay nothing, or very little in income taxes. The penalties for being married or for not being married are eliminated. This approach encourages everyone to purchase healthcare insurance and helps students pay the costs of education. Take your personal data and fill out the following form to see how a flat tax with equal deductions will affect you.

Flat Income Tax Filing Work Sheet

Line #	Line item	Example 2	Example 5	Your Data
1	All Income (pay reported on W2 and 1099 forms, capital gains for investments and/or real estate, dividends, 401 K payouts, pension payments, interest, inheritance, and all forms of income for all of the individuals included as dependents on this Tax Filing.)	50,000	500,000	
2	Number of dependents (Self plus all other claimed dependents, including spouse)	4	2	
3	Standard deduction from income for self and dependents (Line item 2 x $10,000)	40000	20000	0
4	Charitable donations (up to 10% of Line 1 for donations to nonprofit organizations that are on the approved list from the USA federal government)	2,000	50,000	
5	Education expenses (up to $5000 per each individual dependent for tuitions to educational institutions that are on the approved list of USA federal government.)	2,000	0	
6	Mortgage interest deduction (up to maximum of 20% of line 1)	0	100,000	
7	Net taxable income (line 1 less lines 3, 4, 5, 6). If this line is less than zero, then enter zero.	6,000	330,000	0
8	Tax rate (35%)	0.35	0.35	0.35
9	Gross Tax (Line 7 x Line 8)	2100	115500	0
10	Healthcare Insurance tax credit (up to $2000 per each dependent of actual paid health insurance premiums.)	8000	4,000	

11	Total Tax Obligation to USA federal government (Line 9 less line10) If this amount is less than zero, then that is the amount due to the tax payer from the federal government.	-5900	111500	0
12	% of income paid to federal taxes (Line 11 / Line 1).	-0.118	0.223	

This is a flat tax that eliminates class warfare in politics. The wealthy still pay the lion's share of income taxes, and the less fortunate pay nothing because of how deductions are treated. Everyone is motivated to contribute to nonprofit organizations. Contributions from the government to nonprofits can be taken out of the federal budget since people will be doing it on their own. People are encouraged to purchase a home (mortgage), and to purchase some form of healthcare insurance (even if it is catastrophic insurance). And those who cannot afford health insurance are given money from the government as a credit to pay for what they purchase. No purchases are mandated. All are voluntary. Therefore, universal insurance could be accomplished without harming freedom or violating our Constitution.

Chapter 10
Battlefields

Where do conservatives need to fight?

The first rule in winning a battle is picking the correct battlefield. The under-staffed Athenians beat the larger Spartan army by picking a battlefield that kept the Spartans from being able to use their superior numbers. The Afghanistan troops beat the superior USSR troops by not fighting on conventional terrain where the USSR troops could dominate them. David picked a time and place where the reflections of the sun on the shields of his troops would blind the enemy.

Time after time, the battlefield dictated the outcome of the battle.

Conservatives need to take away the advantage had by liberals in the courts, entertainment, schools, and government agencies. Conservatives need to negate the liberal attacks on those battlefields and then force the fight to the battlefields where the conservatives have an advantage.

The bullets in this battle are information. In a firefight, machine guns are placed in positions so they fan bullets in an area with overlap to each other. Then, the target is flanked and surrounded to isolate it. Information must be disseminated the same way. The keys to winning this war are to disseminate information with overlap while surrounding/isolating the target.

The Pew Research Center studied the stories carried on the news of the three most prominent cable stations during the 2008 election. The study did not include editorial oriented shows like Olbermann, Larry King, and Hannity. It focused on just the news shows. This is how these three stations fared at reporting *negative news* about the two presidential candidates.

	Obama	McCain
CNN:	30%	61%
MSNBC:	14%	73%
FOX:	40%	40%

Since NBC owned MSNBC, it is easy to assume that all of the media outlets that were owned by NBC were biased. If you only watched NBC affiliated stations or CNN, then your opinion of the candidates was severely slanted towards Obama. The sitcoms and late night TV did the same thing in their imbedded messages. Since GE owned NBC, it is easy to assume that GE had a stake in the outcome of the election. And it did. GE received a huge share of stimulus money in 2009 and it received unparalleled access to Obama after he was elected. GE did this without any campaign restraints. Its actions were outside of any campaign finance laws. It controlled the news and messages imbedded in entertainment as one big advertisement to help Obama and to disparage McCain.

The media does not have to fabricate news. It does not have to lie. It only has to emphasize the stories that it wants to emphasize and de-emphasize the ones that it wants to hide.

Bernie Goldberg wrote at length about how CBS and the rest of mainstream media do this in his book *Bias.*

On October 21, 2010, NPR/PBS fired Juan Williams as a journalist. Juan had been interviewed on Fox News by Bill O'Reilly. Juan said that he felt uncomfortable when Muslims boarded flights in their full garb. He had some fear about flying with Muslims on his flights. NPR/PBS fired Juan for stating his feelings. And he wasn't even discussing them on NPR/PBS - he was speaking as a guest on FOX. The executives of NPR/PBS said that his views were not within the prescribed attitude of NPR/ PBS. Juan's attitude was not in keeping with the politically correct attitude that NPR/PBS wants displayed as world citizens. Juan had a reputation for blasting conservative policies as a visiting journalist on FOX and NPR/PBS had no problems with that. So while it is OK for NPR/PBS journalists to continually disparage conservatives, it is not OK for journalists to voice an opinion of fear about Muslims.

The firing of Juan Williams sent a clear message to all journalists.

Well, if that were not enough, Juan was fired by a telephone call. A man with ten years of employment at NPR/PBS got fired over the telephone for having an opinion that was different than what was the desired attitude wanted by NPR/PBS.

NPR/PBS is a public media outlet in the USA. It is partially funded by the U.S. government. So what set of attitudes could it have other than those in the Declaration of Independence or the Constitution? What attitude could it have other than freedom of speech?

Well, now it is discovered that one of the largest private donors to NPR/PBS is George Soros. That is the same George Soros who finances MoveOn.org. That is the same George Soros who frequently visits Barack Obama. That is the same George Soros who has benefited greatly from the Obama administration's spending. That is the same George Soros who believes that a world order is more important than USA sovereignty.

Americans have been financing NPR/PBS with their tax dollars only to have NPR/PBS provide bias in how it reports the news to America.

If we the people of the USA cannot trust publically funded media to give unbiased reporting, then how can we trust any media? So what do conservatives do to make sure that the complete truth is really provided to America?

Conservatives should take the fight to the battlefields where conservatives can win. Let's discuss the different battlefields.

The Media and Entertainment —including newspapers

Other than Fox News, the liberals own the media and entertainment. Just like Afghanistan is difficult terrain for a conventional military, the media and entertainment are difficult terrains for conservatives. John McCain made the mistake in 2008 of thinking that the media/entertainment cartel was his friend. He acted as if his witty personality would carry the day. Instead, the media/entertainers killed him - they jumped on every one of his mistakes and emphasized them continually. At the same time, those supposed friends ignored the mistakes of Obama. Pew pointed out that only 14 percent of the stories on MSNBC about Obama were negative while 73 percent about McCain were negative.

What should John have done? He should have used rapid fire to keep the enemy at bay. He should have used quick serious answers; he should have used his media time to attack the enemy. John backed off every issue when he should have been using his media/entertainment opportunities to question every action of Obama. Then he should have used his only ally, FOX, to direct his troops to take action.

For example: John should have challenged Obama's promise to deliver transparency whenever he was on NBC (enemy station) by demanding to see Obama's long form birth certificate, his passports, and his college applications. The issue should have been "transparency." He should have asked on NBC what Obama meant by his comments of "cling to their guns and religion," "my Muslim faith" and "they will call me black." He should have pointed out on NBC how Obama would be the only president in history without operational leadership experience. Instead, John thought that the media would do it ... ha ha ha ... he was naïve. Then John should have used FOX to ask conservatives to demand transparency from Obama. He should have asked conservatives to write to their representatives and senators to demand that the House of Representatives vet Obama to make sure that he never had a dual citizenship as Congress is mandated to do.

John did not understand the battlefields so he did not use them correctly. The mainstream media had labeled him as "mean," so he overreacted to the label and did not attack when he should have. FOX and conservative talk radio begged him for guidance and all he gave them was to "fight, fight, fight."

Compare that to Obama who used the media/entertainment correctly. When on friendly battlefields frequented by liberals— NBC, *The View*, *New York Times*, *The Washington Post*, etc.—he continually used the settings to tell his liberal soldiers what to do—to go out and convince others. He told 75,000 people in the

Denver stadium and millions of people watching his convention campaign speech to go out and knock on doors and to visit their parents and convince them all to vote for "change." And they did.

When working with the media, it is important to treat each one uniquely. Those which are friendly should be used as part of the network to instruct the soldiers on the actual battlefields as to what to do. Those media and entertainment outlets which are enemies should be used to challenge everything about the opponents to cause doubt in the followers of the opposition.

Mahmoud Ahmadinejad was a master of this as he visited the USA. He talked directly to Americans on U.S. media and seriously challenged everything about America. There was nothing cute—or funny—about his delivery. Then on Iranian television, he instructed his public to demonstrate against the American imperialists so that the whole world would take notice.

Friendly media outlets should be used as part of the network to instruct soldiers on the actual battlefields. Those media and entertainers who are enemies should be used to challenge everything about the opponents in order to cause doubt among the opposition.

This is one last point: Stop watching those TV stations that use liberal bias in their TV shows and news. Stop buying products from their sponsors. Stop subscribing to newspapers that use liberal bias in their articles. Do not go to movies or allow your children to go to movies that promote a liberal agenda. Put them all out of business and eliminate the battlefields where liberals like to fight.

Classrooms

Classrooms are battlefields that are owned by the liberals. Colleges, high schools, and grade schools are mostly taught by liberals. As per the data in *Save America Now*, 80 percent of public educators vote for liberals, they belong to unions (i.e., NEA) and they contribute 25 percent of the funds received by Democrats while contributing almost nothing to Republicans. Public educators are government employees. They are the government. Liberal educators teach our children as captive audiences for more than six hours per day and they use that time to conscript our children for their liberal armies.

When *An Inconvenient Truth* was first released, every public school showed it to our children as truth. Now that so much of *An Inconvenient Truth* has been exposed as false or as fabrication, do you see any of our schools rushing to correct their mistakes in the minds of our children? The following article, "The Abiding Faith of Warm-ongers," from Investors.com of December 22, 2010 is representative of the growing amount of information that refutes so much of what liberals presented in *An Inconvenient Truth* and many other misleading documents:

> *Prognosticators who wrote the U.N.'s Intergovernmental Panel on Climate Change, or IPCC, global warming report in 2007 predicted an inevitable, century-long rise in global temperatures of two degrees or more. Only higher temperatures were foreseen. Moderate or even lower temperatures, as we're experiencing now, weren't even listed as a possibility.*
>
> *Since at least 1998, however, no significant warming trend has been noticeable. Unfortunately, none of the 24*

models used by the IPCC views that as possible. They are at odds with reality.

Karl Popper, the late, great philosopher of science, noted that for something to be called scientific, it must be, as he put it, "falsifiable." That is, for something to be scientifically true, you must be able to test it to see if it's false. That's what scientific experimentation and observation do. That's the essence of the scientific method. Unfortunately, the prophets of climate doom violate this idea. No matter what happens, it always confirms their basic premise that the world is getting hotter. The weather turns cold and wet? It's global warming, they say. Weather turns hot? Global warming. No change? Global warming. More hurricanes? Global warming. No hurricanes? You guessed it.

Nothing can disprove their thesis. Not even the extraordinarily frigid weather now creating havoc across most of the Northern Hemisphere. The Los Angeles Times, in a piece on the region's strangely wet and cold weather, paraphrases Jet Propulsion Laboratory climatologist Bill Patzert as saying, "In general, as the globe warms, weather conditions tend to be more extreme and volatile." Got that? No matter what the weather, it's all due to warming. This isn't science; it's a kind of faith. Scientists go along and even stifle dissent because, frankly, hundreds of millions of dollars in research grants are at stake. But for the believers, global warming is the god that failed.

On December 29, 2010, *NewsMax* reported: "For the second winter in a row, icy weather has struck the United States and Europe. Al Gore's global warming theory may be going up in smoke as new data suggests the earth may be cooling, not warming."

Anne Jolis wrote the following in an article posted in the *Wall Street Journal* on February 10, 2011 that was titled "The Weather Isn't Getting Weirder:"

As it happens, the project's initial findings, published last month, show no evidence of an intensifying weather trend. "In the climate models, the extremes get more extreme as we move into a doubled CO2 world in 100 years," atmospheric scientist Gilbert Compo, one of the researchers on the project, tells me from his office at the University of Colorado, Boulder. "So we were surprised that none of the three major indices of climate variability that we used show a trend of increased circulation going back to 1871."

In other words, researchers have yet to find evidence of more-extreme weather patterns over the period, contrary to what the models predict. "There's no data-driven answer yet to the question of how human activity has affected extreme weather," adds Roger Pielke Jr., another University of Colorado climate researcher.

Walter E. Williams made this comment in Townhall.com in January 5, 2011:

In 2000, Dr. David Viner of University of East Anglia's disgraced Climatic Research Unit advised, "Within a few years winter snowfall will become a very rare and exciting event." "Children just aren't going to know what snow is." Britain's Meteorological Office said this December was "almost certain" to become the coldest since records began in 1910. Paul Michaelwaite, forecaster for NetWeather.tv, said, "It is looking like this winter could be in the top 20 cold winters in the last 100 years."

In reference to the last decade of the Earth's cooling, geologist Dr. Don J. Easterbrook, emeritus professor at Western Washington University, says, "Recent solar changes suggest that it could be fairly severe, perhaps more like the 1880 to 1915 cool cycle than the more moderate 1945-1977 cool cycle. A more drastic cooling, similar to that during the Dalton and Maunder minimums, could plunge the Earth into another Little Ice Age, but only time will tell if that is likely." Global warming hype is nothing less than a gambit for more government control over our lives.

In a message dated 2/2/2011 3:35:29 P.M. Eastern Standard Time, JackTymann@aol.com sent this to me:

Gore: Global Warming Causing Record Cold, Snow
Wednesday, 02 Feb 2011 10:06 AM
By Jim Meyers

The record-setting snow and cold afflicting much of the nation in recent weeks doesn't seem to jibe with Al Gore's dire warnings about global warming. But Gore has an explanation for what's causing the wintry conditions: global warming. The former Vice President on Monday responded to Fox News Channel host Bill O'Reilly's on-air question last week: "Why has southern New York turned into the tundra?" O'Reilly then said he needed to call Gore.

"I appreciate the question," Gore wrote on his website.

"As it turns out, the scientific community has been addressing this particular question for some time now and they

say that increased heavy snowfalls are completely consistent with what they have been predicting as a consequence of man-made global warming."

Gore then quoted an article by Clarence Page in the Chicago Tribune in early 2010: "In fact, scientists have been warning for at least two decades that global warming could make snowstorms more severe. Snow has two simple ingredients: cold and moisture. Warmer air collects moisture like a sponge until it hits a patch of cold air. When temperatures dip below freezing, a lot of moisture creates a lot of snow."

"A rise in global temperature can create all sorts of havoc, ranging from hotter dry spells to colder winters, along with increasingly violent storms, flooding, forest fires and loss of endangered species."

It seems that Al Gore and all those scientists who are making lots of money from their environmental grants will blame anything on global warming. And when they cannot blame it on global warming, then they will change it to global climate change.

It seems that these scientists now agree with me. As stated by me more than two years ago in *Save America Now*:

Let me propose an alternate theory to the gloom and doom of global warming; let's says that atmospheric pollution is warming the atmosphere. Then the atmosphere can hold more moisture. So any increase in water levels from melting glaciers is absorbed into the atmosphere. When that moisture saturates the atmosphere, then it rains and that cools the earth and global warming stops. It cools and more ice accumulates—like what has actually happened in Antarctica where there was no flooding. Also, doesn't ice expand to be larger than the same volume of water? What happened to the scientific truth that ice has more mass than water?

It seems that these global warming scientists agree with me, a simple guy with just average scientific education, that the earth will make the proper corrections to itself if global warming does exist. So why don't they say it? Because it doesn't help them justify more government intervention, more government, and more taxes.

Today, more than 60 percent of scientists do not believe that man causes changes to the temperatures of the earth. But, do our children get this message? No. Did our children get any of the information about all of those scientists who conspired to change the data used to prove global warming? No. And why? Because the government is using global warming/cooling/ climate change to implement more control of industry—to interfere with free enterprise. And it needs the teachers— government employees—to turn our children into part of its liberal army of the future to do it.

The government has control of the education battlefield. They use that battlefield to eliminate religion from influencing the values of children, to teach about sex and alternate life styles, to infect children with liberal political beliefs that the children take home to their parents (Obama was extremely successful at this, especially with college students), and to demonize conservatives and private industry.

"We the people" need to neutralize governments' control of the education battlefield. It will be impossible to actually win on the public education battlefields because teachers are with the children unsupervised so much of the day. Even though public teachers (government employees) vote 80 percent for liberals, are more than three-quarters liberal females, belong to the NEA or some affiliate, and contribute 25 percent of all money collected by Democrats; the government advantage in the classroom battlefields can be neutralized. This is how:

1. Work at least three levels above the problem. If a teacher is infecting students with propaganda that is contrary to your wishes, then complain at least three levels above the teacher. In most cases, three levels will be the school board. The school board is elected and is responsible to voters. Don't bother with reporting the infractions to the school administrators... administrators will defend the perpetrator... administrators are part of the problem and probably also belong to the union—so take your complaints to the top.

2. Listen to your children to find out what their teachers are saying. If you ask, your children will tell you everything that happens at school.

3. Vote. Get active in local issues, especially who are on the school board, and help those who think as conservatives get elected.

4. Get your neighbors involved. A friend, Sue will actually write letters that her friends use as templates to send letters to school boards. Every time that she finds something that is in violation to conservative beliefs, she gets at least twenty letters sent to the top leaders who can change the situation. It worked so well locally that now she does it nationally at school districts that are far from her.

5. Change the battlefield. Use alternative education. Cause competition to the government controlled educational system. Home schooling. Private schools. School vouchers. Parochial schools. Parochial schools are actually very cost effective, low priced, with much better education for children. Most religious sponsored schools allow attendance for children outside of the faith without imposing religious doctrine on those children.

6. Decrease property taxes. Most school systems use property taxes to generate revenues to pay for their operations. By cutting property taxes, the funds for public schools are cut. By cutting the size of school systems, the schools have to concentrate on the fundamentals for educating our children.

7. Measure the effectiveness of educators by how the students do on national and international tests and standards. Force teachers to teach about reading and writing and arithmetic rather than spend so much time indoctrinating children with liberal politics.

Your Home and the Neighborhood

Conservatives own this battlefield. While liberals spend most of their time out of the home, conservatives are homeowners, homemakers, and homebodies. While liberals live on caffeine from Starbucks, conservatives gladly walk next door. So bring the battle into your home and into your neighborhood.

We had a very outspoken neighbor who made the accusation that anyone who did not vote for Obama was a racist. As a lawyer himself, he claimed that a legal education at Harvard was enough to qualify Obama to be president, so anyone who did not vote for Obama must be a racist. He stated that Obama's lack of operational experience was racist talk. He got his talking points right out of Saul Alinsky's playbook. He demonized any opposition as "racist." That forced all the neighbors to remain silent, so silence conveyed a message that this liberal lawyer (liberal lawyer is probably redundant) must be correct.

In our Virginia town, most of the wives begged their husbands to be gentlemen and not discuss politics. One day, "the Ripper," another neighbor, made signs in support of the TEA party. All of us except for the lawyer thanked the Ripper. We didn't understand that so many of us were conservatives in support of the TEA party until the "Ripper" finally spoke up. The lawyer got more vocal and the war escalated. He called TEA party participants "tea baggers," which is a very sexually rude and condescending term. Finally, the neighborhood understood the lawyer's demeaning and demonizing tactics and, even though he was a learned man, he was a lawyer.

Conservatives won and the lawyer lost.

Where are good places to have political discussions? In the family room. The living room. The basement. The front yard. The back yard. The kitchen. The dining room. In front of children. While walking the dog. While bike riding. While running. On the tennis courts. On the soccer fields. While playing golf. Anywhere. Everywhere.

Where are bad places to have political discussions? Nowhere.

Even the coffee clutch at church is a good place. Conservatives own this battlefield and need to take advantage of it. Liberals will ask to not discuss politics in the home—leave politics for other places. But do not fall in their trap—liberals want the fight on battlefields that are friendly to them. Conservatives own this battlefield of home and neighborhood and need to bring the fight to it. Often. Loudly.

The Work Environment

As a vice president for a large multinational firm in the 90s, it appalled me how the feminists used the men's fear of feminists to get anything, and everything that they wanted. Men were so frightened of being accused of harassment charges or of not being feminist tolerant that they made many business mistakes that harmed the interests of the stockholders.

Conservatives own the business settings. Conservatives own this battlefield. Any capitulation to conservative principles in business is disloyal to the owners of the business.

Conservatives just need to emphasize what is important for the viability of the business and that will stop the actions of liberals that harm the business. Conservatives to focus on what is important to the business.

- Promotions based on merit.
- Raises based on merit.
- Decisions based on profit contribution, or sales contribution, or competitiveness.
- Good measurement systems with decisions based on those measurements.

Good business practices will stop the intimidation of liberals. Yes, a business needs to be a corporate citizen, but not to the detriment of the business owners.

Then, when the liberals bring up the liberal agenda, conservatives just need to hold fast to what is important to those who actually took the risk to invest in the company. If GM had done this, then it would have never accepted a bailout from the federal government. It would have declared bankruptcy to renegotiate its contracts with the unions. GM executives were traitors to the GM investors and bondholders.

Compare the actions of GM to Ford. While GM was allowing the government to buy the majority of GM and negate the investments of its stockholders, Ford refused the government bailout. While GM capitulated to union demands, Ford reduced costs by replacing many union employees with non-union people and by introducing competitive products like the Ford Edge. Those bond holders and stockholders of GM lost their investments while the stockholders of Ford benefited with a 1,000%—ten times—increase in stock price within two years.

While walking through the aisles of a particular government agency, it jumped out at me that the government employees had Obama and liberal paraphernalia posted in their cubicles during the 2008 election. Then while visiting a couple of very large companies, it jumped out at me how there was no political stuff anywhere.

So why was it okay in a government agency but not in a corporate entity? The government didn't care because Obama was the pick of the government executives. In contrast, the corporate execs told me that they feared repercussions from liberals if they posted their political preferences.

Conservatives, please listen to me. Liberals own the government sites as their battlefields and they use it. You need to stop being so afraid and use the battlefields that you own! It is OK for you to take sides—you are a private entity.

And as for employees, freedom of speech is only as alive as you allow it to be. You can discuss politics at the water cooler, in the break rooms, in the cafeteria, etc.

Courtrooms

Yes, as discussed in *Save America Now,* 80 percent of lawyers vote for Democrats. And yes, most judges were lawyers before becoming judges. So, of course liberals want as many battles fought in courts as possible. They own this battlefield.

The ACLU has intimidated so many businesses and religious organizations into liberal compliance just because those organizations do not want to be dragged into the courts where the liberals control the battlefield. As such, liberals use the courts and the threat of court action to get everything that they want.

This is one of the hardest battlefields to neutralize. But conservatives must not flinch from it. As long as conservatives continue to run from the liberal assaults in the courts, then liberals will continue to beat conservatives with threats of court actions just like a slave owner beats a slave with a stick or a whip.

As a matter of fact, conservatives need to:

- Place conservatives in every elected position that can influence the appointment of judges. Always. And that includes the president of the USA and includes replacing Lindsey Graham.

- Impeach any and all judges that wonder outside of what are acceptable interpretations of the law and state/federal constitutions.

- Seek help from organizations like the Liberty Council that specialize in helping conservative positions in court cases.

- Donate money to those conservative organizations that help conservatives in the courts.

Ken Cuccinelli, Attorney General of Virginia, stands as a perfect example of how to strike back at liberals in the courts. While so many media pundits continue to disparage his attempt to get Obamacare ruled as unconstitutional, he is winning. He may lose, but he put the liberals on notice that they cannot pass laws that are so extremely contrary to basic American principles without someone stepping up and saying that "the emperor has no clothes."

It is up to the rest of us to elect more Ken Cuccinellis, to support them, and to get them into higher offices. That is how we neutralize the advantage of liberals in the courtroom battlefields.

Internet

The Internet was originally the friend of younger people. They have been distracted by Facebook and all the other social uses of the internet. The Internet is clearly now the friend of conservatives. While MoveOn.org—funded by George Soros—was an original place for liberals to go get instructions, it is now dwarfed by NewsMax.com, WorldNetDaily.com, Free Republic, The Drudge Report, Red State, Townhall, The American Spectator, Oath Keepers, AEI, Rasmussen, Liberty, AFP, and scores of conservative sites.

A group of about 100 of us belong to an email exchange group, and many of us also belong to other similar groups. As something happens politically that any of us think should be shared with others, it is sent at the speed of electricity to all of us to be forwarded to others. One piece of information that was deliberately sent by me to monitor its circulation was read by more than a million people within five days and resent to me by a dozen different people from disparate email groups.

In December 2010, the liberals tried to use telephone calls to politicians to push through the Dream Act legislation which would have provided free college education and an accelerated path—a fast track—to citizenship for illegal immigrant minors. Liberals actually sent a phone number (1-866-996-5161) to Hispanics and others that would automatically link them to their senators so they could tell them to vote "Yes" for the Dream Act. Conservative groups got a hold of the number and sent it via Internet to thousands of conservatives to use. Within two days, so many conservatives used it and said "No" to the senators that the liberals shut it down. The Dream Act was defeated.

While the Internet requires an investment of your time, this online battlefield is virtually owned by conservatives. Join sites. Share information. Blog. Do it. And then send emails to any and all government personnel who need to hear from you—senators, representatives, mayors, etc. They all read the blogs at the sites, they have staffers reading the blogs, and they read their emails.

Stay informed. And then help fan the Internet battlefield with overlapping machinegun fire of information. The Internet is all about volume. Ready. Aim. Fire.

Mailboxes and FAX Machines

Mail and Faxes are used so little by the young, blacks, unions, and feminists that they are open territory for conservatives. Liberals are lazy by definition. They want the government to take care of them. Conservatives are individuals by definition, so individual correspondence fits perfectly.

Every single letter or Fax that has ever been sent to a politician by me has been answered within a week. This battlefield is clearly the one that gets most attention from politicians because of the infrequency of use as compared to telephone calls and emails.

To work, each letter must be individual. Names on lists, mass mails, and petitions fall on deaf ears while individually addressed letters and individually worded letters are all read. Keep them short—less than a page at most—preferably less than 100 words. Tell the politician what you want him/her to do and why; Fax is best because it gets there immediately. And one individually written letter means more to a politician than hundreds of phone calls or emails.

A Fax or a piece of mail is a sniper shot. It is a smart bomb. It is a direct hit every time.

Sporting Events

Baseball parks, football fields, NASCAR, golf courses, tennis courts, country clubs—all sporting events—are competitive arenas for individual achievement. Even team sports require individual achievement. By the definition of individual achievement, these are perfect battlefields for conservatives. They are conservative strongholds.

Obama tried to throw out a first pitch at a baseball game and it bounced before it reached the plate. Albert Pujols reached as far in front of the plate as he could. The media deliberately didn't show the actual catch. But all the YouTube videos showed that it bounced. And Obama stood in front of the mound. It wasn't even a full 60 feet. John Kerry tried and it bounced. Al Gore tried and it bounced. President George W. Bush has thrown out the first pitch at scores of games—including the World Series in 2010—and every one of them made it to home plate without a bounce. To throw a good pitch in front of 75,000 people is action under pressure at its best.

Ah, sports and politics. Eighty percent of winning is being there. My tee shirt that reads, "Proud to be an American," would never be worn by a liberal. At sporting events, everyone gives me a high-five when they see it. Wear your conservative symbols. Baseball players and football players wear hats with tiny American flags on the sides. Sporting events start with the National Anthem. Compare that to schools that won't even encourage students to say the Pledge of Allegiance or schools that ban the American flag.

Sporting events are great places to say great stuff in crowds about conservative heroes. This is the time to win easy battles that motivate everyone to take on the liberals. Sporting events reek of macho conservative values. They are tribal rituals and the bon fire in the evening before the big battle in the morning. Use the sporting events to bond—and to have fun.

Lobbies, Bathrooms, Water Coolers, Checkout lines, Movie Theater lines, and Local Restaurants

These are my favorite places to make rapid-fire statements. People are typically standing around and waiting. So it's the perfect time to either say something positive about some conservative action or to take a dig at some liberal. There is no time for rebuttal. It is neutral territory, and it typically makes a point that is contrary to what the liberal journalists have made.

One time, while waiting in line to check into a Marriott Hotel, a young man in front of me made the comment that the government "sucked" in how it was forcing him to purchase health insurance. Everyone around him heard him. His opinion was out there. That little sound bite stuck with me—and lots of others—more strongly than if it had been staged on TV.

The Capital Grill in Washington, DC places copies of the front page of *The Washington Post* on the wall just above the urinals for reading pleasure as you take care of business. One time, a gentleman next to me commented how an article was so misleading that he hoped that the *Post* would go out of business soon. He made his point. He stuck it to the *Post*.

We have a pretty fancy coffee machine at our office. People wait in the kitchen area to use it. Often, someone will comment about something that happened in the news—as when Marco Rubio clobbered Crist in Florida. That comment got Rubio on the radar screen of people who were not paying attention.

Little comments in public places stick to people. They get attention. Silent conservatives learn that others might think like them, that it is okay to speak up, and that the media might just be misleading them again.

And liberals get wounded. Independent voters learn that there are *other* opinions than those that get all the attention by the liberal media/entertainment cartel.

Churches, Synagogues, and other places of Worship

After 6:45 AM Mass one weekday morning before the 2004 election, several of us were conversing in the church kitchen, when the discussion turned to politics. One person said that as Catholics we needed to vote for the party that would do the most good at helping the poor. Then an older gentleman pointed out how many of the government programs that are meant to help the poor get spent on groups that have horrible records at helping the poor. He added that we would be better off donating directly to those who we want to receive help, and getting tax deductions for it. Then a third person spoke up and added that one of the political parties was spending money on things that are in total opposition to the principles of the Catholic Church like Planned Parenthood, euthanasia, and gay marriage. Another person pointed out how politicians were using classic techniques of envy to motivate voters and how envy/coveting is a sin.

These were great conversations. They got more done to implant conservative values on others than any TV discussions could ever do. And it made people think about their core values.

Those were quality discussions. They focused on the vital few items of principle rather than the many items of trivia that liberals try to use to win votes.

Too many in the clergy are more concerned with appeasing people and "compromising" values than in actually discussing the will of God. Too many clergy see themselves as religious politicians. Too many clergy see themselves as moderators of the fight between believers and secularists rather than as soldiers for God. Too many clergy stay silent about the obvious abuses to the laws of God. Too many clergy are afraid to confront the government about freedom of religion and freedom of speech. So it is up to the congregation to do what so many clergy will not do. The congregation needs to fight the fight on the battlefield of the church.

The clergy should be embarrassed that they are not leading this fight:

- To take from one without permission and give to another is theft. It is not charity. It is theft.

- To kill unborn and yet claim that God is the creator at the time of conception is murder.

- To allow divorce for convenience is to allow adultery.

- To allow marriage of same-sex couples and not allow polygamy or marriage to under aged children is hypocrisy.

- To allow envy to be used in politics is to encourage coveting.

- To allow political candidates to draw reference to being the "one," the "Messiah," is blasphemy.

- To deny the impact of religion on the founding of America is to bear false witness, a lie… and a sin.

So speak up at church. What could possibly be a better battlefield to have these discussions than in a religious place?

Chapter 11
A Republic, If We Can Keep It

A woman asked Ben Franklin what kind of government did he and the authors of the Constitution create. He answered:

"A Republic, if you can keep it."

So what is a republic?

WordIQ.com states:

> *Any government that conducts itself under a constitution and the "rule of law" can be loosely labeled a republic... Since the Greek word constitution has been translated as "Republic" one sees the term "democratic republic" meaning a constitutional democracy but really the terms "republic" and "democracy" should not be confused with each other.... The Founding Fathers of the country intended most domestic laws to be handled by the states, although, over time, the federal government has gained more and more influence over domestic law.*

The intent of our founding fathers was to create a rule of law through the Constitution of the United States. They intended for most domestic laws to be handled by the individual states. They created a republic.

That Constitution is the contract between the government and the people. That Constitution limits the authority of the federal government through a check and balance between the legislative branch, the executive branch, the judicial branch, and the states. The authority of the federal government is limited by processes defined in the Constitution, which are meant to be cumbersome to slow down the actions of the federal government, and by defining what the federal government can do and cannot do.

Therefore, Americans need to be wary of anyone who would speed legislation through the process, of anyone who would deny a full hearing about actions by our leaders, of anyone who would add powers to the federal government that are not specifically stated in the Constitution, and of anyone who would encroach on the rights of free speech, religious expression, or gun ownership. The last amendment in the Bill of Rights, the Tenth amendment, is clear:

> *The powers not delegated to the United States by the Constitution, nor prohibited by it to the States, are reserved to the States respectively, or to the people.*

The Tenth Amendment is part of the Bill of Rights. It is a right of "we the people" and the individual states. So violations to that amendment are violations to our rights and to the rights of the state governments. Those violations upset the balance of power between the federal government and the states as established in the Constitution.

Today, many supposed government intellectuals think that there are only three elements to the government balance of power—legislative, executive, and judicial. They forget that the states are part of the balance of power, and that those violations to the tenth amendment are no different than violating rights based on race or gender. They are violations to rights and, today, the federal government—the judicial branch, the executive branch, and the legislative branch—are all in violation to the contracted rights of the states and "we the people." The federal government is breaking the law established in the Constitution. It is destroying our republic.

Henry Lamb is the author of *The Rise of Global Governance*, of Sovereignty International, and founder of the Environmental Conservation Organization. January 8, 2011, he wrote this for WorldNetDaily.com:

The states created the federal government; they designed it carefully to be sure that the federal government could never gain unlimited power to govern as a tyrant. Today, however, the federal government recognizes no limitations on its power; it issues edicts to states and individuals alike, with no fear of retribution. It has gained the power to rule as a tyrant—and does.

Ken Cuccinelli, the Attorney General for the state of Virginia, is a leader of the charge to stop the healthcare "insurance" law from being implemented. He argued a case for state's rights and the unconstitutionality of this law in a federal court. In a letter dated November 29, 2010, Ken wrote the following comments:

Remember that one of the elements of the design of the founding fathers was what we call "federalism." Most people are familiar with the idea of 'checks and balances' in our government, and we usually think of the division of power between the legislative, executive and judicial branches. But there is another division of power within our constitutional system, and that is the division between the federal government and the state governments.

Virginia's own James Madison wrote extensively in the Federalist Papers about how the states would have extensive authority preserved from the federal government to be exercised by the states themselves or reserved to their citizens. When contests about those constitutional boundaries arise, they are to be fought out in our courts, and that is exactly what we are doing in Virginia.

We are fulfilling the founders' expectation of states, that is, because the federal government is overstepping its constitutional authority, the founders expected the states to push the federal government back inside its proper constitutional boundaries, and we are doing that in this case.

I have no doubt which side of this case every single founding father would be on—Virginia's!

Ken needs a lot of good luck to stop the encroachment of the federal government. Think. He is arguing his views in a "federal court." That federal court is part of the federal government. It is not impartial. The federal courts are part of the problem. Even with a positive judgment from the Virginia federal judge, it still will have to go through the federal appeals process to stick.

Since the judge in Virginia and the one in Florida both ruled that the portion of Obamacare that requires all Americans to have mandatory insurance is unconstitutional, it is my opinion that Democrats will conspire with Republicans to repeal Obamacare—or at least the mandatory portion—before the Supreme Court can define the limits to the authority of Congress. As long as the limits are not defined, Congress can stretch its limits. Neither Democrats nor Republicans want limits placed on their authority. Neither party wants to take the risk of such a definition by the Supreme Court. So neither one wants the Cuccinelli case or the Florida case to go before the Supreme Court. Therefore, both parties will conspire to make changes to Obamacare that keep it from going to the Supreme Court.

The losers by this type of cooperation are the American people. What are the limits to Congressional and presidential actions? Who will define them? No one so far.

But to think that the Supreme Court or the federal appellate courts will protect we the people and the individual states from violations by the executive branch or the legislative branch is also insanity. The federal courts are part of the federal government. In the cases brought to federal judges concerning the eligibility of Obama to be president as a "natural born citizen," the federal judges continue to state that "individuals" do not have "standing" to bring such cases. Yet, the Constitution is clear that "we the people" are principles in the contract and that *The powers not delegated to the United States by the Constitution, nor prohibited by it to the States, are reserved to the States respectively, or to the people.*

The people of the United States have standing as individual citizens that federal courts refuse to recognize. The federal government has overstepped its boundaries and the federal courts are complicit.

For example, local governments have always enacted laws that reflect the moral values of the people in those local geographies.

They define such things as adultery, abusive child-care, illegal sex acts with animals, and anything that is important to those people. Recently, the federal courts told the people of California that they could not define "marriage" as only between a man and a woman.

The people of California decided through their defined state constitutional amendment process to define marriage. So what allows the federal courts to negate that? If the people of California can decide that marriage cannot be between a man and a cow, or between an adult and a child, or between a man and several women, then why can't the people of California limit marriage to one man and one woman? What in the U.S. Constitution allows the federal government to negate the will of the people in California on limiting marriage to a union between a man and a woman, but not negate the other limitations and definitions of marriage? Nothing.

The use of "pursuit of happiness" to accommodate gay marriage is inconsistent with the other limitations to marriage. Doesn't a polygamist also have the right to "pursuit of happiness?" The federal courts have stretched the definition of their authority to promote the liberal agenda towards gay marriage. If the Supreme Court agrees with the lower federal courts, then there is no higher court to overturn it. When the Supreme Court acts outside of the will of the people, there are only two other recourses: one, replace the individuals on the court and ask for a new ruling, or two, do as instructed in the Declaration of Independence—which is unequivocal:

> governments are instituted among men, deriving their just powers from the consent of the governed; that whenever any

form of government becomes destructive of these ends, it is the
right of the people to alter or to abolish it, and to institute new
government.

So can we keep America as a republic? Can we continue under the rule of law established by our Constitution the way that our Founding Fathers intended?

Well, the first thing that conservatives need to do is understand that this is a war. It is a war for power to set the course for America. Saul Alinsky understood this. Liberals understand it today.

In the very first chapter of *Rules for Radicals,* "The Purpose," Alinsky used a quote from the Old Testament, Job 7:1, which states: "The life of man upon earth is warfare."

This Is a War

This war is being fought in the courts, in the media, in the classrooms, in the legislative chambers, on the streets, and in our homes. It is about the brainwashing of our children, about causing more dependency on government, and about the deterioration of the Constitution. To win this war, conservatives need to stop the seizer of power from "we the people" by the liberal cartel, by the government, by the New World Order, and by evil people.

The next thing that conservatives need to accept is that there is no middle ground. What is the middle ground between those who think that it is a mother's right to choose whether to keep or kill an unborn child, and those who think that the unborn child was created by God at conception (as stated by the Founding Fathers) with the rights of life, liberty, and the pursuit of happiness as protected by the Constitution?

What is the middle ground between those who think the Constitution provides the method for changing it and those who think they can change it by labeling it a "living document" with interpretations that agree with their political agendas?

What is the middle ground between those that think illegal immigrants are criminals who broke the U.S. immigration laws and those that think illegal immigrants have the same rights as American citizens?

What is the middle ground between those who think the individual is the cornerstone to democracy and those who think that a new world order can supersede any laws of any local government in the guise of UN initiatives or foreign treaties?

What is the middle ground between those who think that the Constitution allows regulation of all monopolies and those who think that union labor monopolies are outside of those regulations?

What is the middle ground between those who think that our rights are determined by God, the Creator, as stated by our Founding Fathers and those who think that our rights are defined by governments?

What is the middle ground between those who think that the size, and influence of the federal government is too large and those who want more government programs?

What is the middle ground between those who think that the job of the president is to be commander in chief of the military and defend and protect the Constitution and those who think the first job of the president is to implement political promises?

What is the middle ground between those who think that the First Amendment provides "freedom of religion" at any time and any place and those who think that the government can impose secularism without that being an establishment of a secularist religious state?

What is the middle ground between those who believe that our USA laws apply to everyone in America and those who permit the use of laws from outside of the U.S. that violate American laws—as when Sharia Law is used in U.S. courts?

There is no middle ground. There is no compromise that does not compromise the traditional values of America. There is no compromise that does not incrementally negate the contract between American citizens and the federal government—the Constitution of the United States.

By removing limits to the powers of the federal government as established in the Constitution, Americans lose a little more control of government each time it is done.

There is no compromise that does not diminish the mission for the U.S. that was established by the founding fathers in the Declaration of Independence.

There is no compromise that does not provide government the opportunity to exploit that compromise at some later time for more than what that compromise was meant to be. There is no compromise between using American laws in American courts and allowing the use of foreign laws in American courts that does not move the USA closer to being part of a New World Order.

There is no middle ground.

The middle ground in tennis is called "no man's land" because you should not play there. If you do, then you lose. If you are in the middle ground, no man's land, then you are not close enough to the net to put shots away, and you are not at the base line to keep shots from being hit at your feet. You lose. A friend of mine likes to receive serves in the middle of no man's land. He is not close enough to the net to put his shot away and he is not back far enough to take a full swing at the ball. Therefore, his little chip shot return allows his opponent to clobber the ball back at him. He loses.

The same is true in business. If you try to straddle between the low cost provider and the functional leader, then you will lose. The big winners in business are either the low cost providers like WalMart or those who provide specialized products like Apple Computers and Nordstrom. The businesses that try to straddle the middle position between product leadership and low price eventually lose.

The same is true in most things. There is no middle ground that is not a loser in the long run. After the compromise, after play in the middle ground, the opponent clobbers the next shot with a shot at the feet, or puts away a shot from the net, or gains product leadership by proving unique product functions, or gains market share by providing a lower price.

Playing in the middle ground is a losing strategy.

So what do we have?

It is a republic, but only if we can keep it. And that means that we cannot accept a middle ground in implementing the dream of our founding fathers.

It is foolish to think that the principles of the U.S. can be compromised without eventually destroying America by continual decay of those principles. The principles of America are established in our Declaration of Independence and our Constitution of the United States. Those who stretch and change the meanings of those documents without the due process for change as defined in those documents are traitors to America.

Our Constitution is what makes the USA a republic. Our republic is what provides the freedoms of religion, speech, and all other freedoms. We are a republic only if we can keep it. And we can only keep it as long as the contract between we the people and our government—the Constitution—is maintained.

This oath is what is stipulated in the Constitution for our political leaders and military leaders: *(I) will to the best of my ability, preserve, protect and defend the Constitution of the United States.*

There is no middle ground. Loyalty must be to the Constitution, to the dream... and not loyalty to political leaders or political parties or political ideology. We have a republic if all Americans force our leaders to keep the oath that they took to preserve, protect, and defend the Constitution of the United States. If you only believe as Edmund Burke did, that "the only thing necessary for the triumph of evil is for good men (and women) to do nothing.... (*paraphrased*)," then conservatives need to take action.

It is time for heroes in white hats on white horses to save all that made America the most wonderful place in the world. We need to save America for our children and grandchildren.

These are the rules:

1. Save

2. Challenge

3. Talk the Talk

4. Walk the Walk

5. Challenge Selfishly

But this is the most important rule for all conservatives:

Make our leaders keep their oaths... make them be oath keepers... hold them accountable to defend and protect the Constitution of the United States... so that each of us can claim to be "doing the work of the one who sent me." (John 5:36)

Works Cited

Articles and BookAlinsky, Saul. *Rules for Radicals*. Vintage, 1971.

Antle, W. James. "Obama Urges Hispanics to Punish 'Enemies,'" Vote Democratic." *The American Spectator*Blog, October 25, 2010.

Armbruster, Ben. "NPR Fires Juan Williams after He Admits Getting 'Nervous' and 'Worried' about Muslims on Airplanes." Think Progress.org, October 21, 2010.

Bellantoni, Christina. "Dems Call On GOPers to Renounce Phyllis Schlafly Over Remarks about 'Unmarried Women' (Audio). *Talking Points*memo, July 29, 2010.

Buchanan, Patrick J. "Who Owns the Future?" Buchanan.org. Blog.

Carrington, Damian. "WikiLeaks cables reveal how U.S. manipulated climate accord." *The Guardian*, December 3, 2010.

Cauchon, Dennis. "Federal Pay Ahead of Private Industry." *USA Today*, March 4, 2010.

Christian, Ernest. F and Gary A. Robbins. "Make No More Faustian Pacts With The Left." Investors.com, December 8, 2010.

Cucinelli, Ken. "Coming this December: A Healthcare Ruling." Cucinelli.com, December 12, 2011.

Edwards, Chris. "Federal Pay Continues Rapid Ascent." Cato Institute Blog, 24, 2009.

El Nasser, Haya and Paul Overberg. "Immigrant population dipped last year, census says." *USA Today*, September 22, 2009.

El Nasser, Haya, Gregory Korte and Paul Overberg. "2010 Census: Slowest growth since Great Depression." *USA Today*, February 3, 2011.

Foster, Peter. "China preparing for armed conflict 'in every direction.'" *The Telegraph*, December 29, 2010.

Fox, Megan. "An Open Letter to Second Wave Feminists: You Failed." News Real Blog, December 2, 2010.

Goldwater, Barry. *TheConscience of a Conservative*. Hillman Books, 1961

Jayson, Sharon. "CDC: Birthrates decline overall." *USA Today*, December 21, 2010.

Jolis, Anne. "The Weather Isn't Getting Weirder." *The Wall Street Journal*, 10, 2011

Lamb, Henry. "The Key to Restoring Lost Freedoms." *WorldNetDaily*, January 8, 2011.

Ledeen, Michael. *Accomplice to Evil: Iran and the War Against the West.* St. Martin's Press: New York, 2009.

Losey, Stephen. "Federal Pay Freeze Plan Wouldn't Stop Raises." *Federal Times*, December 6, 2010.

Master, Michael Charles. *Save America Now*. Dunham Books: Nashville, 2009.

"Insurance Companies are the winners with ObamaCare." *Liquida*, October 8, 2010.

"No. 1 Economic Problem: Not Enough Babies." *WorldNetDaily*, February 6, 2010.

"Peter Morici Gets It." Atlah Media Network, September 5, 2010.

McCarthy, Shawn. "Ted Turner Urges Global One-child Policy to Save Planet." *The Globe and Mail*, December 5, 2010.

Mitchell, Daniel. "The Historical Lessons of Lower Tax Rates." The Heritage Foundation, August 13, 2003.

Morris, Dick and Eileen McGann. "States Taxing Themselves to Death." *The New York Post*, December 23, 2010.

Murray, Shailagh. "In sudden reversal, GOP leader McConnell will back ban on earmarks." *The Washington Post*, November 16, 2010.

Neumann, Jeannette. "Pensions Push Taxes Higher." *The Wall Street Journal*, December 24, 2010.

Pavone, Frank. "Voting with a Clear Conscience." *Priests for Life*(booklet), September 25, 2006.

Perry, Mark J. and Robert Dell. "How Government Failure Caused the Great Recession." *The American*. The American Enterprise Institute, December 26, 2010.

Poor, Jeff. "Scientific American Proposes Global Warming Solution: Birth Control through Contraception and Safe Abortion.Erasing Christianity" Business and Media Institute, October 15, 2010.

Ryter, Jon Christian. "Erasing Christianity," December 24, 2005.

Sammon, Richard. "What to Expect from a GOP House." *Kiplinger*, October 1, 2010.

Sherk, James. "Inflated Federal Pay: How Americans Are Overtaxed to Overpay the Civil Service." The Heritage Foundation, July 7, 2010.

Stein, Sam. "Federal Pay Freeze: Obama Administration Announces Plan To Freeze Salaries Of Federal Employees." *The Huffington Post*, November 29, 2010.

Thompson, Gregory. *Giving Aid and Comfort to the Enemy*.21st Century Press, 2009.

Williams, Walter. E. "Moral or Immoral Government." Townhall.com. December 8, 2010.

"True or False." Townhall.com, January 5, 2011.

WSJ Staff. "Obama: 'If They Bring a Knife to the Fight, We Bring a Gun.'" *The Wall Street Journal Blog, Washington Wire*, 14, 2008.

"Obama tells Republicans to 'Sit in Back.'" *FoxNews*.com, October 25, 2010.

"The Color of News: How Different Media Have Covered the General Election." Journalism.org. The Pew Research Center's Project for Excellence in Journalism, October 29, 2008.

"The Abiding Faith of War-mongers." Investors.com, December 22, 2010.

"Al Gore Shocked by the Great 'Cool Down.'" *NewsMax*, December 29, 2010.

"Fred Smith on the Birth of FedEx." *Business Week*, September 20, 2004.

"Merkel says German multicultural society has failed." *BBC News*, October 17, 2010.

"2001 Flashback: Dems Vote for $1.35 Trillion Bush Tax Cut." *Perspectives*.com. (Blog), January 29, 2009.

Films, Video and Political Cartoons

The Edge of Darkness. Martin Campbell (Director). Mel Gibson (Actor). Warner Brothers & BBC Films, 2010. Film.

The Ten Commandments. Cecille B. Demille (Director). Charlton Heston (Actor). Paramount Pictures, 1956. Film.

CNBC's Rick Santelli's Chicago Tea Party. The Heritage Foundation YouTube Channel. Video clip.

Nancy Pelosi: "We Need to Pass Health Care Bill to Find Out What's In It." Breitbart. tv. Video clip.

Orr, Carey. "Planned Economy or Planned Destruction." *The Chicago Tribune*. 1934. Political Cartoon.

Other Sources

American Rhetoric website

The Art of War (attributed to the Chinese military strategist Sun Tzu)

The Bible (Douay-Rheim and NIV translations)

Bureau of Labor Statistics

The Common Sense Gun Lobby

The Constitution of the United States of America

The Declaration of Independence

Eagle Forum website

Free Republic website

Gallup Poll website

GoodReads.com Quotes

InvestorWords.com

John Christian Ryter website

Ken Cucinelli website

The Liberty Counsel website

Pew Research Center website

Priests for Life website

Rasmussen Reports website

Social Security Administration website

Tea Party Patriots website

The Churchill Center and Museum website

U.S. 2010 Census

WordIQ.com

Zogby International website

Emails

Jack Tymann, Sue Sarkis, dweber2262, Gaven K., John Frase, Dr. Rick Booth, Bernard George and Roanna Brown

Internet Comments

WorldViewDad and "Conservative Coulter Fan"

Conversations

Dr. Jerome Corsi, Peter Morici, Frank Wolf, G. Henkel

About the Author

Michael Master is a former executive and manager at IBM and Amdahl who lives in the Washington DC area. He currently serves as president of a technology firm.

CPSIA information can be obtained at www.ICGtesting.com
Printed in the USA
LVOW071501090213

319421LV00003B/8/P